YOUTH MINISTRIES
Thinking Big with Small Groups

YOUTH
MINISTRIES

Thinking Big with Small Groups

Carolyn C. Brown

ABINGDON PRESS

Nashville

YOUTH MINISTRIES:
THINKING BIG WITH SMALL GROUPS

Library of Congress Cataloging in Publication Data

BROWN, CAROLYN C. (CAROLYN CARTER), 1947-
Youth ministries.
(Griggs educational resource)
1. Church group work with youth. 2. Church group work
with young adults. I. Title. II. Series.
BV4447.B74 1984   259'.23   83-15891

ISBN 0-687-47203-2

MANUFACTURED BY THE PARTHENON PRESS AT
NASHVILLE, TENNESSEE, UNITED STATES OF AMERICA

CONTENTS

PREFACE

HOW TO USE THIS BOOK

This book is for all those people who have cornered me after workshops on education in small churches asking, "What about youth ministry? What can we do to minister *to* and *with* our three, four, or five youth?"

It is also for the members of middle-sized and larger churches who have said, "Hey, do not overlook us. For a variety of reasons, we sometimes find ourselves ministering to and with very few youth. How does a church of three hundred or even seven hundred effectively meet the needs of four or five teen-agers?"

The book grew out of thirteen years of ministering to and with young people in fellowship groups as large as fifty and on an individual basis when there was literally only one teen-ager in a small congregation. During part of this time, I served as Director of Christian Education to a cluster of seven small Presbyterian churches in Orange County, North Carolina. They ranged in size from thirty seven to one hundred sixty members. Some were rural churches—one was a town church in the county seat. Almost all the members of one church were members of the same family. Another was a rural church becoming a suburban church as a city grew around it. During two summers this last church combined forces for youth ministry with the university church downtown. That seven-hundred-member-church ministered during the school year to large numbers of young people. However, during the summer they seldom had more than ten in town. Each of these churches is unique, and each ministers to its youth in unique ways. What they have in common is a seriousness about offering their young people the most effective youth ministry possible.

So, you are not alone. It seems that most churches and church people take their youth ministry seriously. It also seems that there is not much help (books, workshops, etc.) for those with fewer than ten young people who are serious about ministry.

This book does not contain a single, unified answer to your questions. Instead it is a tool kit with which you can answer your own questions in particularly appropriate ways for your congregation and your young people.

Chapter 1 is foundation material. It explores some popular misconceptions about youth ministry that plague those who minister to just a few youth. Once misconceptions are set in perspective, you will be ready to identify what you really want and need to offer your youth. This chapter is essential reading. Do not give in to the temptation to skip over it to a chapter that deals with a more specific concern. The practicalities of the later chapters are based on these first two sections of theory and will be more useful when implemented within the framework provided by the theory.

Chapters 2, 3, and 4 focus on specific types or aspects of youth ministry. Each chapter contains a combination of information and exercises for groups ministering to small numbers of youth. For example, chapter 3 includes a section on "Activities for Small Youth Groups"—a long list of activities for small youth groups and two planning processes to be used by groups in building a calendar of activities.

Chapter 4 is a kit that may be used to design confirmation programs for one or more young people.

Chapter 5 is a process whereby a congregation can evaluate its entire youth ministry. It can be used to tune-up and continually refine a church's efforts to respond to *all* of their youth's needs.

This is not a book to be read and then kept neatly on a shelf for reference. To get maximum results from this book, write in it and even tear it up. Cut out the worksheets.

One person can read this book and work through the exercises alone. However, the book is really designed for use by a small group or committee as it builds its vision of youth ministry and carries out this ministry. The suggested exercises are designed less for teaching about youth ministry and more for planning and carrying out youth ministry. For example, chapter 3 includes an exercise with which a group can evaluate the effectiveness of their youth church school classes, a list of six characteristics of successful teachers of small youth classes to use when enlisting teachers, and an exercise that enables teachers to evaluate their teaching style. These kinds of exercises do not require extra time or work. Instead they offer methods to use in doing the work of youth ministry.

CAUTION: One other important reason to use this book with a group is that one person with a vision might be lonely and not very effective. When two or more share a vision, they become a mutual support team capable of effective action. So read these chapters and try the activities with at least one or two other people in your congregation. Together you can build and implement a vision of youth ministry.

CHAPTER 1

WHAT YOUTH MINISTRY IS AND IS NOT

Real Youth Ministry!?

Over the years—especially the years of this century—youth ministry has developed an image and a place in the life of the church that can bring upbeat joy and can strike awe, even terror. Congregations visibly glow with pleasure and pride as youth are confirmed into full membership or when they take over the leadership of a worship service with poise and youthful creativity. Money to sponsor youth projects is the easiest money the church raises. No other age group in the church has received the focused attention that teen-agers have. More study and program books, films, workshops for youth leaders, and retreats are offered for youth than are offered for any other group in the church.

Yet there is hardly a church of any size that is willing to boast that "we maintain over the years a first-class, lively youth ministry." Many of us can point to a time when "for a little while" or "while so-and-so was here" we had something to shout about. And even when youth ministry is in high gear, most of us enjoy what we see with our fingers crossed, in hopes it will not dissolve before our eyes.

This uncertainty or awe or terror is especially apparent when we seek leadership for youth ministry. Many people who cheerfully do anything else the church asks, and who have the attitudes and talents needed for leaders of youth, balk at the request to teach or work with the church's young people. For this reason pastoral search committees tend to look for ministers who claim interest and skills in youth ministry. Then in turn, when leading his or her growing congregation in calling an associate pastor, most ministers will push for someone to take over the youth ministry responsibilities currently held by them.

Both the joy and the terror are compounded when we minister to and with small numbers of youth. The joy increases because we know each young person individually. So, instead of hearing another fine anthem from the youth choir, we marvel when sixteen-year-old Jo Ann plays the "Hallelujah Chorus" as a piano prelude and recall the Sunday she played "Jesus Loves Me" with one finger on the organ chimes. We are also able to challenge individual youth instead of groups of youth. So, instead of selecting a mission project that can include thirty-five rambunctious junior high students, we are free to introduce thirteen-year-old Thomas, who is raising his first small herd of calves, to the Heifer Project.

Our awe and the terror get further compounded when we begin comparing ourselves to our visions of what youth ministry should be and what we hear about the youth ministry of other churches. When that happens to members of small churches, they lose their self-confidence and begin making lists of all the things they *should* offer their youth but cannot because they are just too small, too limited, and too poor. When it happens to members of large churches with only a few youth, they also lose self-confidence, wondering where all the youth have gone and begin making lists of all the things they *could* do if only they could interest a few more young people.

As our lists of shortcomings and missed opportunities grow, the grandeur of our vision of real youth ministry also grows. Our vision is fed by our memories of every good experience we had at church as youths, the stories we hear about what other churches are doing, the fantastic youth choirs we have heard sing, the aware and able youth representatives (from other churches, of course) we have met at regional or denominational meetings, and articles about youth projects or programs in church magazines. Fully developed, if unleashed on a church concerned about its youth ministry, this vision can be the most destructive force possible. In the face of the vision, we tend to throw up our hands in despair and quit—or just quit hoping.

However, like most of the demons that haunt us, this vision of real youth ministry need not be our undoing. We do need to face up to it. Therefore, an important job for adult leaders in youth ministry is to explore and tame our personal visions. When we ask where we got certain ideas about youth ministry or why we think that certain things are so, we begin to understand our vision. Some parts of the vision lose their power to intimidate us. And we deepen our commitments to other parts of the vision. In the process, the vision becomes a loyal servant and guide instead of an enemy.

On examination we find that our visions are composed of a collection of specific truisms or myths about what real youth ministry is. Most of these myths began as possibilities that worked well. Over the years the possibilities became facts and finally the standards by which we measure our success. They are not, however, unquestionable. In fact, many of the myths include some half-truths and some blind spots along with some truths to be held onto in our visions.

MYTH: Only small churches have small numbers of youth.

The general expectation is that larger churches will naturally include larger numbers of youth and therefore should have larger youth groups, youth choirs, etc. But this simply is not true. Small churches made up mostly of younger families may have larger numbers of youth than the big church whose members are getting older. A church of four hundred members, which five years ago had an energetic youth fellowship of twenty, may suddenly find itself with five or six active youth.

The reason for this is that the size of a church's youth ministry is directly related to the age of the church's adult members and the number of children those people had. Therefore, the size of a church's youth ministry will change while the size of its membership remains approximately the same.

Because of this, *percentages* of youth reached makes a more realistic standard than *numbers* of youth reached. Thus, a large church that includes mainly young adults or retired adults need not apologize for supporting only a lively youth fellowship for their ten teen-agers.

Churches of all sizes may be faced with ministering to and with small numbers of youth.

MYTH: Great youth groups go places together on buses.

On the surface, this myth looks harmless enough. Busloads of happy, singing, cheering teen-agers are a common sight. For years, churches have sent busloads of young people to conferences, work camps or retreats. Many adults fondly remember the bus trips of their own youth years and wish such experiences for young people today (although they hope they will not be asked to chaperon). That is all well and good unless your church has no hope of filling a bus or even a van with its youth. In that situation we can bemoan what we cannot offer our young people, or we can look at what makes bus trips so special and create something else that provides a similar experience.

Bus trips are special because they take youth to new experiences. Youth see new places, meet new people with new ideas at conferences, try out different types of Christian service, and live with people in life situations that are very different from their own. Such trips also provide youth with time to be with people their own age in a relaxed atmosphere. None of this depends upon the bus itself or the twenty to thirty necessary to fill a bus. Four or five youth with their advisor can reap all the benefits in a car. In fact, because it is easier and cheaper to arrange for a carload than for a busload, a small group is able to travel more frequently. All that is required is an adult leader with a vision of youth ministry that depends on carloads instead of busloads.

What we do and where we go with young people are more important than the mode of transportation used to get there. A carload—even in today's small cars—can benefit from traveling together as Christians.

MYTH: Great youth groups play volleyball.

There is hardly a book for or about youth ministry that does not include at least one picture of youth playing volleyball. Because it is a high-spirited game that requires limited athletic skills and tends to build group solidarity, volleyball has become the unofficial game of youth ministry. But volleyball requires a minimum of six players and really isn't much fun until you have ten or twelve players. Given this limitation, it's easy to jump to the conclusion that until you can fill a volleyball court, you cannot have first-rate youth ministry. So what is a group of five to do?

A small group can play half-court basketball or four-square or other games that require fewer players. Successful youth groups do play active, inclusive games together. In fact, groups that do not play together regularly tend to be rather drab—they also miss out on a rich opportunity in ministry to youth. But there are other high-spirited active games besides volleyball (see chapter 3's "Recreation" for some examples).

Youth ministry includes recreation for whatever number of youth are available.

MYTH: Successful youth groups love to sing together—in beautiful harmony—accompanied by guitar-playing youth or their leaders.

The vision of youth singing around the campfire or choirs of youth singing enthusiastically in worship services is especially attractive to most adults. Indeed, there are many songs such as "Pass It On" and "They'll Know We Are Christians by our Love" that seem to belong especially to young people. Adults whose own youth predates rock music and television can hardly imagine a youth gathering that does not include such group singing.

But it is a fact that just any group of any size cannot do such singing. Group singing requires at least one strong lead singer—especially if the group is small. It also requires the enthusiasm of the majority of the group. In today's world where young people tend to listen to music rather than to sing it, such leadership and enthusiasm is the exception rather than the rule. This situation is further complicated by the self-consciousness most youth feel about their singing.

It is one thing to sing when your voice is lost in the chorus but something else to sing when everyone can hear your voice. So, group singing will only occasionally be part of the youth ministry that includes a small number of youth.

But—that does not mean we are not doing youth ministry if we cannot sing together. Singing is only one of many activities we can offer youth ministry. There are limitless others: studying, worshiping, creating dramas, creative arts, service, and even clown ministries. The real truth in this myth is that only some youth groups (mainly larger ones but also some smaller ones) find group singing a meaningful part of their life. However, it is equally true that there are plenty of successful youth groups that never sing a note together. Neither one is better than the other. They are just different.

There is more to youth ministry than group singing.

MYTH: Every church needs a youth group.

The definition of *youth group* may vary in its details, but basically it refers to a regular meeting of teen-agers with adult advisors for study, fellowship, and service. The problem with this myth is that it assumes that the only way to do youth ministry is to have a youth group. That is not true. It is quite possible for a church to effectively minister to and with a small number of youth on an individual basis without forming a group. This may be necessary in suburban churches whose youth attend different schools and live in different areas. It may be equally necessary in a church whose youth are all brothers and sisters or at least cousins. (Chapter 2 outlines ways to undertake youth ministry other than by forming a youth group.)

Youth ministry is more than providing a youth group.

MYTH: Youth ministry is something that happens on Sunday night at church.

One popular way of doing youth ministry that developed during the middle of this century was the Sunday evening youth fellowship at church. It began at a time when churches were moving away from having Sunday evening worship services, but when people still wanted Sunday to be holier, quieter, and different from the rest of the week. Sending the youth to church for an evening of study, worship, and fellowship geared especially to their interests was a good way to deal with youthful energy, while preserving the sabbath. This Sunday evening youth group idea worked so well that it became almost synonymous with youth ministry.

But times change. Sunday evening may be the most inconvenient time to gather young people—especially in the summer. People camp, travel, and play on the weekends. Therefore, it becomes important to meet youth groups after school or to plan for several retreats a year instead of weekly meetings. Making such changes is not giving in to youth or parental demands. It is not settling for second-class youth ministry—even if the church is quiet on Sunday evening. Instead, such changes respond to a new situation in a way that takes advantage of new opportunities.

Youth ministry is living out and sharing the gospel with young people, as we minister to the needs of youth and to the world with our youth. Sunday evening youth groups are only one of many ways of engaging in youth ministry.

MYTH: If a church offers meaningful youth ministry, young people will invite their friends and the group will grow. (Stated in the reverse: if your youth ministry does not include growing numbers of youth, it's a failure.)

This is a particularly difficult myth to cope with because it contains a goad that we can neither ignore nor focus on completely. The truth is that we are called to minister to people of all ages—including teen-agers. Any time we are content to minister only to those young people who come through our doors of their own will, we need to reevaluate what we are doing. On the other hand, the main purpose of youth ministry is not to see how many young people we can coax into our programs and projects, but what to do with who we have.

To keep a proper balance between these pressures, adult leaders in youth ministry need to have a clear picture of how many youth are part of their church, how many youth are part of other churches in the area, and how many community youth have no church connection. In some rural areas and small towns, almost every young person has family ties to a church. In such areas, youth groups, no matter how successful, seldom grow beyond the members of their own congregations. Such groups need not despair when they are not growing or even when they are shrinking. The percentage of available youth being reached is a more useful and realistic standard than the number reached. A church that involves five of the seven teen-agers on the roll need not be intimidated by the churches that include seventy-five of the one hundred twenty-five teen-agers on their roles. Bigger is not always better in youth ministry.

By now you may be identifying other myths that belong to the particular vision of youth ministry that haunts you. We all struggle with many of the same myths, but each one of us also copes with a few unique myths that grow out of our own experiences. The more clearly we understand these myths, the more easily we can harness their power to serve us, instead of hinder us.

One characteristic of the destructive myths of youth ministry is the implication that there is only one right way to do youth ministry and that any church that cannot or will not do things in that way is failing. The myth makes us think that if our youth do not sing or we cannot fill a volleyball court or no one goes to the annual youth conference this year, then we're not doing good youth ministry. The fact that youth taught most of the classes at Bible School, that two young people are serving on church boards, or that all of the high school students spent two days at a vocational counseling center at church expense count for little if they are not part of the local myth about the right way to do youth ministry.

In its most demonic form, this idea that there is only one right way to do youth ministry traps us into worrying about survival of groups and being sure certain events and programs take place. It is demonic because the proper focus of real youth ministry is not on programs but on people. Our chief concern is to enable young people to grow in their faith and discipleship. Our guiding question is not "How can we keep our youth programs alive?" but "How can we minister to and with these particular young people?" Because all people are unique, no one program is right for all. The right youth ministry program for the young people of one church is all wrong for the group in another church. The programs and plans that are perfect in a church one year may be totally uncomfortable the following year.

This means that adult leaders must be constantly alert to the needs and opportunities their young people face. The vision that guides us best is a vision of our particular young people, the world in which they are growing up, and the God by whom they are called. Therefore, the next section is devoted to exploring what (if not groups, volleyballs, and programs) youth *do* need from their churches to keep them growing in their faith through their teen years.

What Do Youth Need from Their Church?

Once we have set aside some of the myths about what youth need from their churches, we need to answer the questions about what youth really need. What is our responsibility to the teen-age members of our congregations? What do they need from us to keep them growing in their faith? When we have the answers to these questions clearly in mind, they become the heart of our vision of real youth ministry. Therefore, it is worth the time and effort to answer carefully.

What do youth need from their churches in order to keep growing in their faith? They need . . .

A GROUP IN WHICH THEY ARE LOVED

Some sage has said that teen-agers focus their entire lives around only two questions: (1) Who am I? and (2) Do they like me? This sage further points out that for teen-agers, the second question is the more crucial of the two. The teen-age years are a time of sifting through all that everyone else is wanting ME to be and trying to mold ME to be. The purpose of this sifting is to decide what I want ME to be and to begin being that person. That is without a doubt one of the most responsible tasks we tackle in our lifetime. It is also very scary.

Fear is what makes that second question so dreadfully important. All alone a young person makes a brave decision about who he or she wants to be, and then immediately begins checking for signs of what others think of the decision. For example, if the decision is to be an athlete, the teen-ager almost frantically begins checking for signs of what others think of him or her as an athlete. Does she make the team? Do friends laugh at his jogging plan or admire him? And how do the important adults in her life respond? Are they proud of the victories, sympathetic with the defeats, and supportive of all the work? In short, do they like ME, the athlete?

Building ME involves not just sports but how I will dress, how I will treat friends and enemies, what I think about the issues of the day, what kind of job I want to pursue, what values I will make most central, how I treat people of the other sex, and endless other concerns. Because building ME is so all-encompassing, the teen-age builders need enormous amounts of reassurance and support from as broad a group as possible.

The church can be this group. We are a community of people who believe that each individual is important to God and loved by God. When we translate that belief into action, we become a group that loves each person—warts and all. When we love youth in this way, we . . .

—know them as persons. We call them by name and talk with them about things in which we know they are interested.

—listen intensely when they talk, expecting that what they say will be worth hearing. We do this listening constantly.

—appreciate the skills they offer and the person they are now, rather than what we see them becoming. We communicate this by asking them to use their skills in the work of the church now and by letting them know we like them.

—provide opportunities for young people to spend large amounts of time with other teen-agers doing a variety of interesting and fun activities. Building a ME requires constant testing out of possibilities. Most of this testing must be done in a group. A loving church provides as much of this time as possible.

—stand by them when the ME they are trying out at the moment is offensive to us. The person who knows she is loved no matter what she does is free to try and discard many different ME's in the process of settling into lifelong patterns with which she is secure and happy.

Few groups in the world are able to give teen-agers this kind of love. Many families even fail to do this. So, the church that loves the young people in its midst with this kind of love is giving them a rare and precious gift that will shape their entire lives.

FRIENDSHIPS WITH ADULT CHRISTIANS THEY CAN KNOW AND EMULATE

As teen-agers go about the business of creating their own ME, there are many powerful pressures being put on them to influence their work. Advertisements tell them how they ought to eat, dress, act, and brush their teeth. Friends tell them what they like and dislike. Teachers at school tell them what they will and will not accept in certain areas. In short they are bombarded by conflicting messages about what they ought to be.

One common way of coping with these messages is to select one or more heroes to pattern ME after. The church needs to provide as many as possible of these Christian heroes. The best of these heroes are not distant ones (like visiting Christian athletes) but well-known adult Christians in the local church. These heroes need not be perfect Christians. It is more important that they be people who are still growing in their own faith and will admit that to teen-agers. They need to be people to whom young people feel free to turn for help with personal problems and questions. Such people offer young people a vision of a Christian ME to grow towards.

ENCOURAGEMENT TO ASK QUESTIONS, THINK, AND SEARCH OUT
THE MEANING OF LIFE

While childhood is largely a time of becoming familiar with the world and how it works according to adults, youth is a time of evaluating everything that was previously accepted at face value during childhood. Youth is a time for questioning everything and everyone in order to decide "what I think, what I value, and how I will live." This process can be frightening for young people (in spite of outward shows of grandiose self-confidence) and jarring at best to their adult friends who must watch them tear apart everything the adults hold dear.

But it is crucial for the church to give its approval and even blessing to the process. Adults must encourage the questions, listen thoughtfully and non-defensively to the doubts, and share the struggle. This is no time for pat answers or memorizing the catechism. It is a time for pondering the mysteries, admitting the unanswerable questions, sharing insights and meaningful experiences, listening to untested ideas, and searching out the meaning of life together.

To offer this kind of encouragement, churches must provide youth with teachers, pastors, youth advisors, and adult friends who understand this need to question and doubt and who will respond supportively to the young people as they do it.

A CHANCE TO BE THE CHURCH TODAY

As they become independent during the teen-age years, young people learn less and less by *studying about* and more and more by *trying out*. It is a time for learning by *doing*. Therefore the church needs to offer young people more opportunities to *be* the church than to study about it. Youth need to plan, lead, and participate in worship. They need to identify mission concerns and become directly involved in them. Service projects, field trips, youth choirs, work camps, youth lay readers, youth Sundays, and youth representatives are the order of the day. The more parts of the church's life they are actively involved in, the more teen-agers will know about the church. In the process they will also have opportunities to try out many potential parts of "ME, the Christian." They can try out "ME, the committee member," "ME, the teacher," "ME, the helper-servant," even "ME, the preacher."

EXPOSURE TO THE RICHNESS AND DIVERSITY OF THE WHOLE CHURCH

As our young people are learning about the church by being the church, we must take care that their vision of the church is broader than what goes on in a particular congregation. Youth have both the mental ability for, and the interest in, exploring and evaluating the larger church in all its richness and diversity. Because of their natural curiosity and thirst for new experiences, we should introduce them to as much of the church as possible.

Small church youth and large church youth need to meet each other to learn about the similarities and differences in their congregational lives.

City kids and country kids need to introduce each other to their Christian communities.

All youth need to experience our great variety of worship styles: grand choirs and elaborate rituals, gospel singing, communion served in pews, around the table, or at an altar rail, house church worship in a basement play room, special seasonal worship, and much more.

Youth need to learn how the larger church does its business, including visits to watch deliberating bodies in action, work camp tours of mission projects, and even visits to denominational offices introduce youth to the scope and methods of the church's work.

All of this provides young people with a clear picture of what our church is. With this information, young people have freedom to create a unique Christian ME that reflects all the church is. They also begin viewing that unique Christian ME as part of a much larger community that shares in its rich diversity a common faith.

TO SEE THEMSELVES AS CHRISTIANS

In many ways, this is the final step towards meeting all the other needs. As young people create their own ME, we as a church need to challenge them to make some definite decisions about what part the Christian faith will play in their life. The church encourages children and youth to learn and grow in the faith. But, there comes a time during the teen-age years when the church must step back from promoting its faith in order to challenge its sons and daughters to decide what they personally think and want to do about all they have seen and heard and experienced.

This decision can be the focus of confirmation. For most churches, confirmation is the time when a person assumes responsibility for his or her own faith. In some denominations it is linked to believer's baptism. The timing of this special event is crucial. Though arguments are offered in support of setting confirmation for every age from seven to twenty-five, there is a growing consensus that the mid-teen years may be the best. Between fourteen and sixteen, young people are making important decisions about their identities and futures. They are choosing school courses that lead to college or jobs. They are deciding which jobs or professions they want to follow. Some are beginning serious relationships with potential spouses. They are ready and able to make an intelligent decision about Jesus' call and to follow up on the commitments their decision implies. Therefore, the church has a responsibility to clearly challenge them to make this decision, support them as they make it, and stand by them whatever they do decide (even if they decide they are not ready to make the decision).

Churches that provide serious confirmation programs rather than a perfunctory ritual offer their young people the chance they need to decide to be a Christian.

All together, this task seems like a lot to ask—especially of a small church. It is—but look again. Most of what is needed is recognized in warm, caring human relationships. Youth need people to love them, adult Christian heroes to look up to, and people who will support them as they ask their questions. What group is better qualified to provide these relationships than a small church where everyone is known by name? Other youth needs point more to the nature of youth activities most churches provide rather than to any exotic new programs. Youth need a chance to be with other youth, a chance to air their doubts in an accepting atmosphere, exposure to the larger church, and a challenge to decide about their faith. This says more about how we handle church school, what we plan for confirmation activities, and how we involve youth in the daily life of the church, than about new programs we ought to add to our schedule.

To evaluate your effectiveness in meeting the needs of the young people in your church, answer the questions on the following page. Answering the questions with a group of adults interested in your church's youth ministry would be more helpful than answering them alone.

HOW WELL ARE YOU MEETING THEIR NEEDS?

1. How do you love your teen-age members?

   A. List everyone in your church between the ages of twelve and twenty:

   B. What percentage of the adults in your church could complete "A"? _____ percent

   C. Check the statements below that are true of your congregation:

   _____ Adults are frequently seen talking with teen-agers in friendly conversation about personal interests.

   _____ Teen-agers are generally listened to here. They have good ideas!

   _____ Our teen-agers know they are loved—no matter what they do.

2. List adults in your church with whom several youth have close relationships and whom they admire:

   Are you happy to set these people before youth as examples?
   What got these relationships started?
   What could you do to encourage more of these relationships?

3. List ways your young people do the work of the church today:

4. True or false?

   _____ Leaders in our church school classes and other youth groups are more interested in encouraging young people to do their own thinking than in getting them to give the "right answers."

   _____ Our young people know at least two people in our church to whom they would feel free to go to discuss personal problems and serious questions about the Christian faith.

   _____ Our confirmation program really challenges young people to make a decision that both the congregation and the young people take seriously.

5. List activities during the last year that have involved your young people in the life of the larger church beyond your own congregation:

CHAPTER 2

REAL YOUTH MINISTRY WITH INDIVIDUALS

Meet some growing teen-age Christians.

CHERYL is a budding musician. At fifteen she plays the piano and the flute quite well. For several years she has played occasional piano preludes for worship. The volunteer organist works with her to select appropriate music. Last summer Cheryl took over while the organist was on vacation. She and the pastor selected hymns to go with the worship themes.

CLAIRE has participated in the annual CROP walk for two years. This year she served as her small church's recruiter (with adult support). She recruited walkers, made a poster or two, got a friend to make the announcements in worship (she is quite shy), and collected the money.

GEORGE is an all-American fourteen-year-old. He plays football. He also has a gentle, sensitive side. An alert adult in his church recruited George to become a "big brother" to a difficult, disruptive six-year-old. For a while George attended the grades 1-3 church school class with the task of helping young Chris get along better. He also visited Chris at times and took him to a carnival at church expense. In the process, George enjoyed being Chris's hero, developed his own skills as a caring, loving Christian, reduced but did not end Chris's disruptiveness, and ministered to Chris in a way no one else could.

AMANDA was literally the only teen-ager in her church. But she was also vitally interested in her faith and her congregation. At fourteen she began teaching the three children in the children's class. One of the parents who was also a public school teacher helped Amanda get started and provided lots of moral support, along with answers to her questions about teaching. The church paid her way to an occasional workshop.

MICHAEL at seventeen is a thinker and a student. He wants to become a writer. He periodically visits his pastor to have long, deep discussions about his ideas. The pastor loans him an occasional book to read and discuss. Michael wrote a senior English paper based on one of these discussions.

JANETTE'S parents were going through what could only be called a messy divorce. Her pastor let her know he was aware that the divorce was rough and had created some pretty tricky problems for her. He checked in with her occasionally to see how things were going. She called when she needed someone to talk to.

JOHN is a born leader. He is president of his class and participates in dozens of clubs and projects. He is one of seven teen-agers in his church. His church school teacher suggested him for membership on the denomination's area youth council. He served this year as president of the council.

SARA was not a member of the one hundred forty member congregation. She came to occasional youth events when she was thirteen or fourteen. At seventeen she came to a couple in the church asking to move in with them. Her family had become unbearable. Sara had more than a few problems, but the couple welcomed her and worked with her. A church neighbor gave her odd jobs to make some money. A lawyer in the congregation represented her without charge in a brush with the law. Other parents in the congregation supported the couple as they attempted to respond to Sara's needs. During the year she lived there, she seldom attended any church function.

These young people are growing in their faith under the care of a congregation that includes fewer than ten teen-agers. Their needs are not met by groups or programs but by caring adult friends who make the effort to know each young person well enough to offer challenges, opportunites, and resources on an individual basis. In such churches, teen-agers are regular attenders at Sunday worship, may have a church school class, and participate in church projects and fellowship events. They are more often in intergenerational groups than in groups of youth. To effectively conduct this type of individualized youth ministry, a congregation has five tasks:

(1) **The church must make all gatherings, events, or projects that include participants of all ages truly inclusive.** Such events must not be adult functions at which youth and children are tolerated because there is nowhere else for them to go.

If Sunday worship is the major weekly congregational activity in which youth are involved, then that worship must be responsive to the worship needs and concerns of youth as well as of adults. The beginning of the school year, exams, getting along with friends, dealing with conflicts, and family problems need to be regularly included with adult concerns in congregational prayers. Sermons must include illustrations from the world of youth. Occasionally, the message of the sermon may be more youth-oriented than adult-oriented. Sermons will need to be presented in a variety of ways that catch the attention and imagination of listeners of all ages. (Slides, dramatic readings, and stories appeal to all worshipers. Lectures generally appeal only to adults.) Youth can serve almost any role adult lay people serve in worship. Therefore they need to be included as lay readers, ushers, and greeters just as adults are.

Youth who join regularly in such services have opportunities to hear God's word read and applied to their world, to share themselves with God in worship, to develop a picture of "ME, the member of God's people." Many of their needs for growth can be met in such carefully planned worship services.

If the main opportunities for youth to be involved in Christian mission are the mission efforts of the church, then those efforts must be planned to include young people. In planning regular and special missions we must constantly ask, "How can we include the young people in this?" So, for example, if your finances are based on pledging, then teen-agers should be asked to make and keep pledges. Setting aside part of their money, whether it is from an allowance or from their own earnings, is a very real part of their development as Christian stewards. The church needs to encourage this in many of the same ways it chooses to encourage adult stewardship.

HOW DO *YOU* INCLUDE YOUTH??

1. List below the major all-church events and projects in your congregation during the last year. Include annual events, one-time events, and ongoing activities.

    Worship
    —weekly worship

    Mission

    Fellowship

2. Identify ways youth have been involved in each activity. Where are they simply tagging along? Where are they enthusiastic participants? In what ways have they been included in planning and carrying out these activities?

3. Review your list again to identify some specific ways you could make each event more inclusive of youth.

Much of the mission work customarily done by adults can include young people. Young people can participate in collecting old clothes from their own closets and those of their friends. They can pick up clothes from other members to take to central collection points. They can work with adults on sorting and packing clothes for shipping. When school is out, they can work with adults to deliver "Meals on Wheels" (on snowy days such sure-footed help is especially appreciated). Their energy and ability, when combined with adult know-how, can tackle almost any manual work from repairing old homes to adding on to the church building. They can share in visiting older members accompanied by an adult. They can work with the pastor in planning and leading communion services for the homebound or institutionalized. We should remember the young people and ask them to join in work in which they have interest and for which they have ability. They can be and need to be doing the work of the church today.

Even social events can be inclusive of young people. Not only can teens be involved in serving meals, but their interests can influence what programs follow the meal, how the church will celebrate its one-hundredth birthday, and what will be planned for the Christmas party. Youth often learn how to be good committee members as they work on church committees planning such social events.

(2) **The church must respond to both the needs and the abilities of each young person.** Each of the young people described at the beginning of this chapter has a unique set of needs and talents. Their congregations know them well enough and care about them enough to respond to their uniqueness. Very few youth have needs that are beyond the resources of even the smallest caring congregation. Even troublesome, troubled Sara could have gotten little more from a church with extensive youth programs than she did from the small group of folk who did so much work on her behalf. Chances are she might have gone unnoticed in a program-oriented congregation. And what pastor of a big church has time for impromptu philosophical discussions with a Michael—even if Michael had the guts to come past the secretary to the inner office?

Churches with few youth programs can be successful in developing talents. Had Cheryl, the musician, participated in a church with well-developed youth programs, she would have enjoyed membership in a youth choir with professional leadership. There may have been a handbell choir to try out. Some time during her church school years, she would have related certain hymns to particular scriptures. She would have encountered and enjoyed a rich variety in church music. But she also would have been one in a crowd. There would probably be several other young pianists as good as she. Therefore, she would develop only as a member of the musical groups. She would not get the individual attention, the opportunity to shine, and the encouragement. On the other hand, in her individual-oriented church, she will probably learn and retain more as she and the pastor select hymns for the next Sunday's worship than she would in a church school class on hymns. She will see herself more clearly as a contributing member in ministry to the congregation and her Lord than she could as one member of one of three choirs.

Sara, Michael, Cheryl, and countless others are living proof that churches can effectively minister to youth on an individual basis. What is needed is alert, caring adults who know the young people well enough. These adults are equipped to suggest that a Cheryl take music leadership, or to mention a Claire as leader of a mission project, or to give a Janette the extra loving hugs and TLC she needs as her family crumbles.

(3) **The congregation needs to note publicly important events in the lives of its young members.** Big events such as graduation may merit a gift presented publicly and even a party. Smaller events such as prizes won, getting a driver's license, going on a special trip, or being invited into an honor group all deserve mention. In larger congregations this means posting news clippings on the bulletin board and mentioning them in newsletters. In smaller congregations the events in the lives of members of all ages can be mentioned from the pulpit and included in the church's prayers. Such public recognition, when added to comments in casual conversations, tell a young person he is cared for and important in his congregation.

WHAT ABOUT *YOUR* YOUNG PEOPLE?

Divide a large sheet of blank paper into four columns.

(1) In the first column list each of the teen-agers in your congregation, leaving space between the names. Check the rolls to be sure you include everyone.

(2) In the second column, next to their name, note all the ways each young person is ministered to and ministers with the congregation. This should include activities participated in, special relationships with adult friends, and responsibilities.

(3) In the third column list the unique abilities/talents that young person has to develop and to use as a contributing member of the congregation.

(4) In the last column identify personal needs to which the congregation could be responding.

SAMPLE

Name	In the church	Abilities/Interests	Needs
Charlie	—fairly regular at church school —Sunday worship —sings in choir —led recreation at Bible school —makes & keeps a $ pledge	—friendly —liked by people of all ages	—chances to develop leadership skills —inclusion in some happy families (home is unhappy)

(5) Review your work. Compare the abilities and needs of each person with your description of their involvement in the church.

In what ways are you helping them develop and use their talents as Christians? What could you do to encourage them further?

How well are you meeting their needs? How could you as a congregation and adult friends be more helpful?

(4) **Young people need to be led into participation in youth events sponsored by the broader church.** Most denominational regions sponsor youth events such as retreats, conferences, summer camps, travel camps, work camps, mission/travel camps, and rallies. These opportunities contribute to almost every need for Christian growth. As youth meet other youth and visit other Christian communities, participants develop knowledge and appreciation of the richness of the wider church. Quality leaders often become heroes to imitate. New experiences and late night discussions encourage searching questions. Youth like John, the leader, find a larger group of Christian youth where they can develop their abilities. And the warmth of the fellowship at such events draws all young people deeper into the loving Christian community. Many adults point to such youth events as experiences that have shaped their entire lives. Visions were formed and lasting commitments were made.

Getting young people to attend such events is not as easy as it looks. It takes some careful thought and persistent work. Public announcements about these events are generally mailed to the pastors of all congregations in a denominational area. Unfortunately, such notices often never get past the pastor's desk.

So the first task is to get these announcements into the hands of some adults who will (1) read them, (2) decide which youth, if any, in your congregation might be interested, and (3) encourage interested youth to participate.

This last step is the biggest job. Basically it includes informing youth of the event, offering financial assistance when needed, checking on transportation needs, and getting registration forms in on time. But, if the youth in your congregation have never gone to such events, the job requires lots of gentle urging. The events must be described in great detail. Phone calls encouraging a young person to go have to be followed by phone calls asking if "you've thought about it" and "will you let me register you?" These trips look awfully risky to teen-agers the first time they try them. Sometimes youth will only go to such a first event if a trusted adult from their own church goes along also. Sometimes it helps to work into such events slowly, trying out an all-day rally, then a weekend retreat. After that most youth are ready for a week or more. As a general rule, the more area events youth have been involved in, the easier it is to encourage their participation in others. The job of the adults becomes seeing that each young person gets the information about appropriate events and providing appropriate congregational support.

This is a job for the pastor or any interested, willing adult who knows the young people and can converse with them comfortably. The more the young people like and trust this adult, the easier and more successful the task will be in the early stages.

(5) **Congregations also need to direct their young people to services that are available to them through the larger church.** For example, many presbyteries work in partnership with presbyterian colleges to provide vocational counseling for high school juniors and seniors. During a two day visit to the guidance

WHAT DOES THE BROADER CHURCH OFFER *YOUR* YOUTH?

Before you can direct your young people to events and services sponsored by the broader church, you have to know what is available. To make a list of what is available to your particular youth, contact one or more of the following:

—your pastor
—a Christian education staff person on your district, presbytery, or conference staff
—a professional church educator in a neighboring church of your denomination

Once your lists are complete, write the names of youth who are taking advantage of each event and service. If you do not know this information, ask your young people.

SAMPLE LIST

(This is the list of events and services available to churches of Orange Presbytery in North Carolina. Marginal notes show how one church with twelve teen-agers makes use of those services and events.)

Activities/Events

annual Jr. High retreat— *5 went this year*

annual Sr. High retreat— *John + Al*

Day in the Sun
(July picnic with recreation
& music)

summer camps— *church budgets to pay fees as needed*

denominational youth— *sr. highs will go for the first time this summer*
conference

synod Sr. High retreat

Services

Vocational Guidance— *church pays for each junior to have this experience*

Family Life Center
(counseling)

College catalogs for all
denominations' schools

center, students take interest and aptitude tests that they discuss with trained counselors. They use a library of vocational materials to explore vocations identified as having potential for them. Local churches often pay part or all of the cost of this service for their young people. Adults in churches who minister to individual young people need to know what services are available to their youth and how to get those services.

When these five tasks are thoughtfully carried out on behalf of the young people in the church, a congregation has a right to take pride in the real youth ministry they offer. They are meeting the needs of their young people in ways that take full advantage of the kind of caring Christian fellowship the congregation is.

CHAPTER 3

REAL YOUTH MINISTRY WITH SMALL GROUPS

Small Church School Classes

Every church does not need a youth church school class. It is possible for a young person to be ministered to and to do ministry in a congregation without joining a church school class. A person can grow up in a church to become a responsible adult Christian without the benefits of a youth church school class. We all know this.

Still, most churches will work hard to provide youth church school classes for a variety of reasons. "We've *always* had one," some say proudly. "A *good* church *ought* to have one." "It's our responsibility to our youth," others chime in. "We've got to keep our youth active. They are our future. If we lose them now . . ." In some situations an honest parent might add, "We've got to have something for them to do during the hour other family members are attending classes."

But these kinds of reasons rise from the demonic visions of real youth ministry that are not based directly on providing what youth need to keep growing in their faith during their adolescent years. Church school is only two hundred years old. It was not invented until the eighteenth century. For over seventeen hundred years, Christian young people passed through childhood and adolescence and into adulthood without church school. Neither Martin Luther nor John Calvin ever heard of or attended Sunday school, yet they managed to grow into remarkable Christian maturity.

So when we talk about youth church school classes, our first question must be, "What is their purpose?" In what way will a church school class help our particular young people to grow in their faith?"

If we refer to our list in chapter 1 of the needs of youth, almost every need listed could be met at least in part by a church school class. The class can be a group where a young person experiences love. A good teacher often becomes a very influential hero. Classes should certainly encourage thinking and asking questions. They may offer youth a chance to do the work of the church today as a class. Church school can be the gateway through which young people are introduced to the larger church. Through church school a person may come to see herself or himself as a Christian. But no one church school class can do all of it. The list of needs is too long and too diversified, and church school time is too limited.

Therefore a congregation must designate specific needs to which church school is to respond. Two or three needs is the most a class can seriously tackle. One or two other needs might be met in a limited way as a fringe benefit. For example, a group that focuses on thinking and questioning and on exposure to the church might, in the process, become a group where students feel expecially loved.

Once a congregation has a clear sense of what it is trying to accomplish with young people during church school, it is ready to begin designing a class or classes that will do the job. Designing requires decisions about the size and shape of classes, descriptions of the kind of educational activities they will pursue, and descriptions of the kind of teachers the classes will require.

WHAT NEEDS DOES YOUR CLASS MEET?

Below are listed the needs of youth for Christian growth. For each of the youth church school classes, do the following:

*—mark the needs that you believe the class meets completely.

○—circle the * of those needs that you think are intentionally met.

✔—check the needs that are to be met in church school, according to church stated purposes.

    —a group in which they are loved.

    —friendships with adult Christians they can know and emulate.

    —encouragement to ask questions, think, and search out the meaning of life.

    —a chance to be the church today.

    —exposure to the richness and diversity of the whole church.

    —to see themselves as Christians.

Ask yourself:

1. Does each church school class have a clearly defined purpose?

2. Is our church school class(es) meeting the stated purpose?

3. Is your congregation asking the youth church school classes to do more than is possible? Less than it is capable of?

STOP NOW. Do NOT begin redefining the purpose of your church school classes. These purposes must be defined in relation to all other aspects of your congregation's youth ministry. Chapter 5 will deal with that. For now continue building your understanding of small youth church school classes as you work through the rest of this chapter. This will prepare you to plan more ably for a church school that is an integral part of your total youth ministry.

SIZE AND SHAPE: WHO WILL BE IN EACH CLASS?

One of the main barriers to success for small youth classes is the idea that real classes have at least ten students (and the best ones have fifteen to twenty-five students). This idea developed as public schools and large church schools were attempting to keep classes from becoming too large. Their question was, "What is the largest class in which effective education can occur?" Unfortunately, their answer that the best classes included fifteen to twenty-five is often interpreted not as an upper limit but as an ideal size. Based on that misinterpretation, churches with fewer than ten youth tend to bemoan their inability to provide good church school classes for their youth. We ignore the fact that the private schools advertise their small classes, and colleges boast of their low teacher-student ratio. Instead of bemoaning our size, we could be rejoicing. We can boast of three to five student seminars! It's all a matter of attitude.

Once we have decided that classes of fewer than five students are interesting, lively possibilities, the question of how we group youth for classes becomes real again. Should ten teen-agers be one class or two? On what basis do we divide them?

Answers may be based on several truisms.

*Younger teens and older teens study more effectively in different groups. The difference in both the interests and the academic skills of a thirteen-year-old and a seventeen-year-old are enormous. The seventeen-year-old has reading, research and critical thinking skills beyond those of the thirteen-year-old. Furthermore the seventeen-year-old is much more aware of the world. Therefore, three or four younger teens with a teacher and three or four older teens with their teacher will learn much more effectively than six to eight teens, aged thirteen to eighteen, in one class could. This is especially true when the purpose of the church school is study.

*One way to group classes for study is to follow public school groupings. Students move into the younger youth class as they enter the junior high or middle school. They later move into the older group when they enter high school. If most of a congregation's youth attend the same school system, this provides a basis for the unity of each class. It does not work as well when the youth attend schools with different grade groupings.

*Classes can be grouped around natural friendship lines. Children often form close groups of church friends that are easily recognizable. The bases of those groups vary widely. In one small church there was a clear break between the older brothers and sisters and the younger ones. At the meeting point were two girls in the same grade in school. However, one was clearly identified with the older group and the other with the younger group. Each one had a brother or sister in the other group. That church recognized that natural division and planned classes accordingly. In another church, the division was naturally created by a two-year-period during which no children were born.

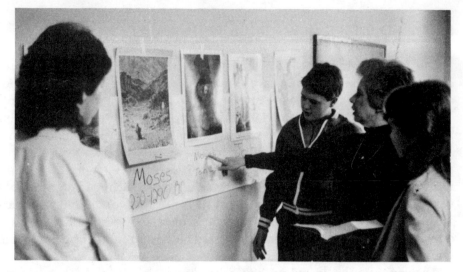

TEACHING STYLE: WHAT WILL THE SMALL CLASSES DO?

There are two basic styles of education: (1) lecture and (2) student activities. Both are useful styles. Each one, however, works better in some situations than in others.

The lecture style is more appropriate in large groups. The student activity style is more comfortable in smaller groups. The lecture style is often an efficient way to communicate new facts. The student activity style allows students to investigate, experiment, and evaluate new ideas and ways of understanding. The lecture style de-emphasizes the personal relationships between teacher and students. The student activity style enhances and is enhanced by strong friendships among the teacher and students—therefore for a small youth church school class, the best style is the student activity style.

The classes in the student activity style can be compared to college seminars. A small group of students (the smaller the better) meets regularly with their professor to work on case studies, discuss and solve problems, critique each other's work, and submit their growing knowledge to the evaluation of the group. The professor does not lecture in a seminar. She poses problems, presents cases for study, and asks questions to help students develop their thinking. Most college students find that good seminars are one of the most exciting, stimulating parts of their college education. The best small church school classes I have seen are seminars on the Christian faith. Two to five teen-agers meet weekly to explore their growing Christian faith by working through student activities planned for them by their teacher.

These activities include everything from biblical research using adult study tools to dramatic reading and to self-expression using creative writing and art. Younger youth especially enjoy projects that involve creating replicas, and using somewhat sophisticated art media. Many older youth, unless they consider themselves artistic, tend to shy away from using many art media, unless equipment such as cameras and recorders is involved.

The element that is shared by all of these activities is a high level of student participation. Though the teacher usually selects the activities and directs the action, the feeling of the class is, "We're all in this together." The teacher is less the sage with the right answers and more the coach leading the team in discovering answers. Student ideas and suggestions are taken seriously. Listening in on such a class, one hears students talking as often or even more often than the teacher speaks.

I have compiled a list of teaching/learning activities for small youth classes, which is long but could be even longer. You may immediately think of activities that are omitted—add them. New activities can also be created by combining several on the list. For example, a class of two or three younger youth could create a television documentary presenting some biblical event. In the process they would have to do some research and study, create a script, maybe plan a dramatized interview, and videotape their documentary. There is almost an endless stream of possible classroom activities for the small class.

TEACHING/LEARNING ACTIVITIES
FOR SMALL YOUTH CLASSES

Reading in class
—individuals read
 silently
—one reads aloud as
 others listen
—one reads aloud as
 others follow own
 copy
—students read aloud in
 turns

filling in study charts
together

filling in work sheets
individually

making banners

photography
—taking pictures to use
—selecting pictures to
 use

illustrating prayers,
scriptures, poems,
hymns, etc.

creating write-on slide
slideshows

debating an issue

writing
—diaries
—prayers
—poems
—paraphrases of
 scripture
—letters to officials on
 matters of concern

research using dictionaries,
commentaries,
concordances, etc.

discussions

field trips

viewing filmstrips

studying and making maps

making mobiles

making models (example:
ark of covenant)

making a movie, videotape
or slideshow

listening to and discussing
music

singing along with
recorded music

making posters expressing
their ideas about a topic

preparing puppet shows

dramatizing a story

interviewing a guest

dramatic reading

making timelines

working puzzles
(crossword, hidden
words, decoded
messages, etc.)

planning own worship

together trying different
ways of praying

playing games to practice
skills (example: races in
answering questions
using study tools)

doing value clarification
exercises

working through case
studies

listening to mini-lecture
(five minutes maximum)

listening to illustrated
mini-lecture (seven
minutes maximum)

study/action projects

OTHERS?:

WHAT DOES YOUR CLASS DO?

If you teach a small youth class, read the list of Teaching/Learning Activities for Small Youth Classes:

—Put a ✔ by each activity done in your class in the last month. (Add ✔'s for each time you have done an activity.)

Ask yourself:
1. How many different activities have we used this month?
2. Do we overuse any activities? If yes, what other activities on the list might accomplish the same learning?

—Put a * by each activity you personally would enjoy.
—Put an X by each activity you personally would prefer to avoid.

Ask yourself:
1. Which *'ed activities are not ✔'ed? How could your class use these activities next month?
2. Have you X'ed any activity that is also ✔'ed? How much do your personal preferences limit the activities in which you lead your students? (Do not be too hard on yourself. Every teacher avoids particular activities. But good teachers work to keep the activities they avoid to a minimum.)
3. Which *'ed but seldom ✔'ed activity would you like to learn how to use confidently? Ask your pastor to help you locate workshops or books on this classroom activity.

If you plan for a church school that includes a small youth class, use the list to:

—evaluate potential curriculum. As you skim a unit, note every suggested activity. Then ask yourself if there is a good variety of activities. (CAUTION: This is not the *only* test for curriculum.)

—ask teachers to respond to the list as suggested above. Help them locate resources to develop new teaching skills they indicate in the last question.

—identify the equipment, books, and supplies that are necessary for each activity.

Be sure as many of them are on hand as possible. Find sources for items not on hand.

Be sure teachers know where to find all this.

LEADERS: WHAT KIND OF TEACHERS ARE NEEDED?

By now it is becoming apparent that the selection of teachers for small youth classes requires careful consideration. We know what we want the class to accomplish and how we want the job done. We need teachers who teach in a given style and relate to youth in a need-meeting manner. As we seek these leaders, we must be aware that there are some skills any interested person can learn and certain attitudes that can be developed or curbed. But behind these there is a set of personal characteristics or dispositions that seem to mark good teachers of small youth classes. These attributes can be polished and refined. But, if they are not at all evident in a person by nature, there is little hope that they can be created from scratch.

CHARACTERISTICS OF SMALL YOUTH CLASS TEACHERS

(1) **Small youth class teachers like and enjoy teen-agers as people.** They consider teen-agers people who are worthy of their attention and friendship. They appreciate the problems teen-agers cope with daily and expect both integrity and creativity in their solutions to the problems. They keep in touch with youth music, sports, fashions, and interests. They laugh at junior high jokes.

(2) **Small youth class teachers are more concerned with what their students learn than in themselves as a teacher.** In other words, they are less interested in their role as teacher than they are in their task of teaching. It's a subtle but important distinction. The teacher who only focuses on his role has some ideas of what a teacher ought to be and do. When this teacher is in the classroom, he works on being and doing things that fulfill this role. Any activity that does not fit the role will be avoided. On the other hand, the teacher who focuses on the task of teaching will try just about any activity or media that might help students learn. This teacher can be relaxed and freewheeling because there is no role to protect.

(3) **Small youth class teachers affirm the value of the individual.** They really believe that when two or three or even one or two have gathered together, important things, like good Christian education, can occur. They put as much time and effort into preparations for their two or three as any teacher devotes to a class of twenty. And, they do not consider their efforts in any way wasted on so few. Though they work hard to get all potential students to attend, they show no disappointment on those Sundays when they work with only one student.

(4) **Small youth class teachers are more interested in promoting student thinking than in hearing right answers.** They allow young people space to state their doubts without censure and to try out their developing convictions without fear of ridicule. No topic that is of real concern to the students is too absurd or too sacred to submit to group scrutiny under the teacher's leadership. Such teachers recognize the need to question and doubt and investigate before one can truly believe.

(5) **Small youth class teachers teach in the participatory rather than the lecture style.** It's a fact that the lecture style simply does not work in a small class. It is also a fact that it is very hard for a teacher who always uses and prefers the lecture style to change their style. Therefore, it is unwise to recruit such a teacher for a small youth class, hoping that they will make the change when they see the need. It is best to recruit a person who prefers the participatory style.

(6) **Small youth class teachers are comfortable sharing themselves with youth.** They let their young friends get to know their real ME—warts and all. They put their ideas on the table for group evaluation along with student ideas. They can accept and value student analysis of their ideas. They offer themselves as older Christian sisters and brothers who are still growing in their faith, and show by example that much is gained when we each share the joys and trials of our growing.

This is a large order. However, most churches, even the smallest ones, include several potential youth class teachers. They simply have to be identified and supported.

NOTE: Even the smallest class is best served by two teachers. On most Sundays there will be only one on duty. But two are available for driving on field trips and special activities. Also, having two on the team provides comfortable sharing of responsibilities, vacations that do not interrupt the class, and knowledgeable substitutes to cover last-minute absences.

SPACE: WHERE THE CLASS MEETS

It would seem that three or four youth and one adult could meet just about anywhere—and they can. But they do need a few things.

The class needs a table(s) and chairs. Review the list of teaching/learning activities. How many require tabletop workspace? Lounge furniture or upholstered sofas are not the seating for this kind of work. One or two tables of the kind you can sit around or work on are needed. The closer the table is to square or round, the better. (Full participation is encouraged when students sit in a circle or square so that each one can see all others.) The class needs some shelves or cabinets for safely storing their supplies and equipment.

This furniture can be found or arranged in almost any room. Four or five can work together on the kitchen table using the counters as extra work space and one section of a cabinet for storage. In a crowded building, two or three can even meet around a small table at the end of a hallway (during the week their table is set against the wall and their materials stored in a box under the table). A larger class can meet in a wing room of the sanctuary, pushing their table against the back wall to make space for rows of chairs during worship. Or a group can meet at the front of the sanctuary using the front pew for seating along one side of their foldaway table. A class might even have its very own room in an education building.

Ideally, the amount of space used should feel comfortable for the number of people meeting in it. Avoid space where the group is too cramped to move around comfortably. If you must use a room that is too large, mark off an area within it as yours. Use bookshelves or tables to create an artificial wall. An area rug can mark your boundaries on the floor.

Many classes must share space with a group that meets at another time. It may be the scouts (in the hall), or the women (in the kitchen), or the worshiping congregation (in the sanctuary). In such cases the class needs a way to safely store their resources and supplies in a convenient way. This may be a cabinet, some shelves, a file cabinet, or a box.

Wherever the youth class meets, the youth need to have full ownership of the area during their meeting. People walking through, women "slipping in to check on the coffee," the organist, or those arriving early for choir rehearsals are unacceptable interruptions. Post signs, make public agreements, and enlist the support of your superintendent and pastor to end such interruptions. If this is not successful, find other space that the youth can have total possession of during their allotted time.

When a congregation states a clear purpose for youth church school, carefully forms classes in the manner of a seminar, staffs those seminars with selected teachers, and provides appropriate space, exciting educational opportunities generally result.

One year the three teen-agers in one small church became the church school teachers for the children's class. One evening each month, they met with their teacher to study (on their own level) the subject they would be teaching the children and to plan their lessons. Their teacher did not attend the children's class on Sunday morning unless she was asked to come by the young teachers. During that year the children enjoyed their young teachers and studied hard under their leadership. The student-teachers were pleased with the church's confidence in them and happily claimed that they learned more as teachers than they usually did as students.

In another church there was a seventh-grade girl who felt too old for the children's class, but was definitely not yet ready to join the youth class, which at the time included mainly older youth. So, she was given a self-instruction book that surveyed the Bible. She worked happily through the book in a little study carrel set up for her in a corner of the children's class. After each class the children's teacher checked on her progress, helped with questions, and offered encouragement. For her at that time, this was exactly what she needed to keep growing in her faith.

These churches and others like them, offering educational opportunities that take advantage of the small number of young people involved, have a right to be proud.

Activities for Small Youth Groups

This part of chapter 3 and the next one both deal with youth fellowships or youth groups. I use these terms broadly to include any groups of youth who meet regularly under the church's care to study, play, and serve together. (They do not, however, include church school classes.) These groups may be called MYF, PYF, youth club, or a name chosen locally. They meet at times other than Sunday morning and tend to be more informal than Sunday morning activities.

This section focuses on what such groups do and how they find the program resources they need. It deals with programming. The section entitled "Patterns for Small Youth Groups" outlines several patterns for small youth groups and describes ways leadership for such groups can be provided. It deals with organizing.

Each section is necessary to complement the other because both careful programming and effective organizing are related and equally important. If you do not plan and select a program carefully, you run the risk of organizing a group doomed to fail because it does not respond to needs, or fated to succeed at accomplishing nothing. It is hard to say which of the two is worse. On the other hand, programs that are a perfect match to the needs of your youth can fail if they are not organized and carried out in an effective way.

Most churches faced with ministering to small numbers of youth begin with questions about programs.

"WHAT CAN WE DO? WE'RE SO SMALL!"

One frequently heard wail from youth advisors is, "But what will we do? There are only three regular members. That is not enough to do anything, is it?" To answer that question turn to the end of this section to the list titled "What We Can Do." This list is subdivided into five lists. Each of the five includes activities related to a specific aspect of the Christian life: worship, study, ministry within the congregation, service (beyond the congregation), and fellowship. Together they include activities encouraging every kind of Christian growth.

---

1. Read through the entire list, placing a ✔ by each item that could be done by three young people with one adult leader.

2. Draw a line through each item that is totally impossible for a group of this size.

3. Put a question mark (?) by each item with which you are unfamiliar.

4. Review your marked list.

   —Count the number of items you ✔'ed.

   —Are more items ✔'ed or crossed out?

   —If you are doing this with a group, compare your lists of unfamiliar items. Share with each other what you know about items others have ?'ed. Either check or cross out items as you learn about them.

This exercise points out emphatically that small youth groups have an almost endless list of possible activities to consider. They can do almost anything a group of ten or twenty or fifty can do. They can do some of them more easily and effectively than the larger groups can. All they need is the support of a congregation that believes that three or four youth (1) are worth ministering to, and (2) can prform worthwhile ministry. Once again, it is a matter of attitude.

"OK, THERE IS A LOT WE *COULD* DO.
BUT ON WHAT BASIS CAN WE DECIDE WHAT WE WILL DO?"

A youth group needs a purpose or sense of direction. Advisors, youth, parents, and the church boards need to share a common vision of what the youth group is to be and do. When the group plans, it can then select activities to carry out this purpose.

This purpose is most usefully defined in relation to other aspects of the church's youth ministry. The church school class, youth groups, confirmation programs, choirs, and all other youth ministries need to be planned so that each one complements and builds on the other. No one class or group can meet all the needs of the young people. But if they are carefully planned, they can.

Therefore the only way to answer the question, "On what basis can we decide what we will do?" is to define the purpose of your particular youth group in relation to the total youth ministry of your particular congregation. Chapter 5 provides a process for that decision making.

"NOW, WHAT WILL WE DO NEXT WEEK?"

There are two ways to respond to that question: (1) order a youth group curriculum, and (2) do some planning with your young people.

(1) **Order a youth group curriculum.** Several denominations produce quarterlies with a program for each weekly meeting of a youth group. Many of the items on the "What We Can Do" list are included in these programs.

The strength of these curricula is that they answer the question "What shall we do next week?" and tell you precisely how to do it. For adult leaders who are working with a youth group for the first time, this provides some security. For adult leaders who are busy, it provides programs requiring limited preparation.

The weakness of these programs is that youth groups using them can slip into the suggested pattern of devotionals, business, and program until it becomes a dull ritual. If the content and style of teaching the youth group curriculum are nearly the same as those of the church school curriculum, the youth group becomes a second church school class. Consequently, instead of meeting a different set of youth needs, a congregation ends up overconcentrating on one set of needs while ignoring the others. Generally, this means that youth get more study and worship than they really need and fewer chances to do the work of the church today.

In the final analysis, the prepackaged format that is the curriculum's greatest strength is also its weakness. It provides support to adult leaders by making many of the decisions about what a group is going to do. But in so doing, it denies the young people the chance to learn and grow as they are involved in making those decisions.

(2) **Do some planning with your young people.** Involve them in deciding what they want to do to keep growing in their faith.

Planning is not easy. Ask any group of any age, "What do you want to do?" and most of the time a long, uncomfortable silence will be your answer. Most people do have ideas about what they want and need to do, but they need help getting those ideas out and discussing them with a group.

"HOW CAN OUR GROUP PLAN EFFECTIVELY?"

There are a variety of processes that help people plan effectively. There are two somewhat similar ones that have proven useful in planning with small youth groups.

Either one of them is used by a group of young people gathered to make plans for their group. They may plan for any span between four months and a year. Planning for a year enables long-range preparation but can leave a group committd to an activity they are no longer interested in eight months after it sounded great. Planning for four months often does not provide enough preparation time for major activities and may leave the feeling that "We are always planning." One compromise is to plan in six month chunks but always be open to planning for major events more than six months away.

Both of the planning processes require several hours of work at one time. At the minimum, a group must set aside a long afternoon and evening with alternating periods of work and play. An even better situation is a two-day overnight retreat. Neither process can be handled effectively in two separate one or two hour meetings.

(1) **The Planning Deck.** Before the planning session, the adult leader(s) creates a "deck of cards." Each card in the deck describes in a phrase one activity the group could do together.

To develop the deck, the adult leader(s) gathers a list of activities that fit the designated purpose of the group. Use every possible source. Pick items from the "What We Can Do" list. Think of ways the youth could become more involved in your church's life and work. Find out about area youth rallies, retreats, and conferences. Make your list as varied as possible.

To make the deck, divide sheets of paper into eight equal sections as illustrated. In each section write a one phrase description of one activity. You will need one deck for each planner. The easiest way to duplicate the deck is to use a photocopier. If you do not have access to a copier, make several copies at once using carbon paper. After making your copies, cut the sheets into cards.

Separate the cards into piles of related activities. You may pile them according to the needs they meet. You may select the titles of the lists in "What We Can Do" that are related to the stated purpose of your group. Or, you may devise your own categories such as (1) explore, (2) serve, and (3) play.

Give your planners one section of the deck at a time. (It is often easy to start with "fellowship.") Ask each individual to read each card, then to place it in one of three piles: (1) YES! I'd like to do this!, (2) MAYBE, and (3) YECH! I do not want to do this!

When all the piles have been formed, ask each planner to read his "YES!" pile. Any card that is on every "YES!" pile is automatically placed in the group's "YES!" pile. Repeat the process for the "YECH!" pile. Then offer time for discussion of the remaining YES's, YECH's, and MAYBE's. The group may decide to add any of these to either their "YES!" or their "YECH!" pile. Encourage individuals to campaign for activities they would like to try. When discussion is winding down and your "YES!" pile appears completed, set aside all cards except those on the final "YES!" pile. As a group, select three or four of these "YES!" cards as top priorities. Draw a star on each of these cards.

Then hand out another stack of cards and repeat the process. Do not get bogged down. No matter how many stacks you have, the process for all of the stacks should take no more than forty-five minutes. When you finish the last stack, take a break. You all deserve it!

At this point you should have spread before the group all of the selected activity cards, some of which are starred priorities. The next step is to arrange your chosen activities on a calendar. It is best to use a wall calendar with large blocks for each date. Begin by writing on the calendar those activities with pre-set dates or seasonal emphases. Then, fill in with other activities, starting with the starred ones. Remember, some activities will take several weeks. Others may be set at times other than the regular meetings. Avoid making plans that will conflict with other church, community, or school events. But do not get bogged down. This will have to be a flexible calendar. As time progresses, changes will have to be made. For now, be content to have identified projects, set a few specific dates, and sketched out some general blocks of time for given activities.

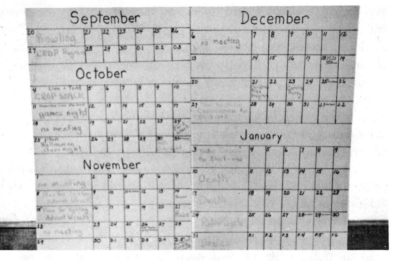

(2) **Brainstorming.** Ginny Ward Holderness in *Youth Ministry: The New Team Approach* outlines a brainstorming process for planning in youth groups. The process assumes that the group is to pursue a balanced selection of activities in worship, study, ministry within the congregation, service and fellowship. She parenthetically suggests some adaptations for smaller groups using the process. When those adaptations and several others are made you have the following process:

Before the session, tape on the wall five sheets of newsprint or five brown paper grocery bags cut open with grocery logos taped toward the wall. On each sheet write one of the following titles:

> Worship
> Study
> Ministry within the congregation
> Service beyond the congregation
> Fellowship

Also gather two or three marking pens.

When the planners have gathered, explain the five types of activities you will be planning and outline the overall process. Then, select one of the five kinds of activities. (It may be easy to start with "fellowship." Or, you may want to start with "worship" and move through the other four in order.) Have copies of "What We Can Do" available. Together begin brainstorming a list of possible activities in the selected area. Write each idea on the wall list.

The rules of brainstorming are (1) that every idea is accepted no matter how way-out or unusual it sounds, and (2) that ideas are accepted without evaluative comment. This is not the time to say, "that is ridiculous" or "we could never pull that off." Instead—this is time to get as wide and wonderful a view as possible. Dreaming is allowed and even encouraged because what at first may be dismissed might be seen later to be quite realistic. So—brainstorm!

To get their thoughts going, planners will want to refer to the appropriate section of "What We Can Do." New planners will probably end up choosing items from these lists. More experienced planners will use the lists as jumping-off points. When the group is out of steam on one list, move on to the next until you have lists for every area. You may want to take a brief break here. However, if enthusiasm for the possibilities is running high, go on to the next step.

Now is the time for some thinking and selecting. Work on one list at a time. Discuss some of the more interesting and some of the less familiar items on the list. How could they be done? What would they accomplish? What difficulties would they pose? Together create a picture of what would be involved in the activities. But do not get bogged down in details. As soon as the group shares a vision of the main activities on the list, ask each individual to select three items for inclusion in the group's plans. As each planner reports his three votes, mark them on the paper. Circle the top three or four vote-getters. These become the group's priorities. Repeat the process for each list. Then, be sure to take a break. This is hard work!

Regather to build a calendar. Have a wall calendar with large blocks for each day. First write on the calendar those activities with pre-set dates or seasonal emphases; then place the other activities. If several sessions are required for an activity, set them aside. For example, a group might devote three sessions to preparations for a haunted house to raise money for UNICEF at Halloween. That group would need to set aside most of October for this work. There will be time for little else. As you build your calendar, maintain a balance of activities throughout the year. Avoid long runs of any one type of activity. Some variety is pleasant for everyone. Again—do not get bogged down. This calendar will have to be changed throughout the year to adapt to unforeseen conflicts, new opportunities, and snowstorms. It is a starting point that you will want to post in your group's meeting area.

Both processes work well in small groups of youth. Each has its strengths and weaknesses. The card deck demands a lot of leader preparation. Making the deck is time-consuming. Copying it and cutting it up is not fun. But it does provide young people, who have never had an opportunity to plan their own activities, a good beginner's process. They can focus on selecting from what is available rather than

inventing possible activities. For such youth, the brainstorming process may be overwhelming and frustrating. However, experienced planners enjoy the permission to dream that brainstorming offers. Often they come up with ideas no one had considered and prove them to be workable and worthwhile. Interestingly, the "What We Can Do" list can be used year after year. Each time it is used, young planners notice an activity they skipped over before or identify a new angle on an activity they have already done. Last year's study of clowning ministry may lead to developing a clowning program for a local rest home this year.

Using these planning processes can be a very exciting experience. The group generates great expectations and enthusiasm. But several days later, adult leaders reviewing the planned calendar will probably experience dismay.

"THOSE ARE GREAT IDEAS! BUT WHERE CAN WE GET THE RESOURCES TO REALIZE THEM?"

How do we go about planning a Youth Sunday worship service? Where are we going to find program materials on clown ministries?

Most people can manage the service and fellowship activities. We know what to do or where to go for help on these. It is the worship and study activities that concern us most. In these areas help is needed with the content and the way to explore that content with students. Do not dismay; there is lots of help available. All you need to know is where to look for it.

Places to Find Resources for Youth Ministry

(1) **The library and curriculum storage closet at your own church**—There may be nothing there, or you may find a small gold mine. Aware of the planned activities, skim contents of youth curriculum. (Do not ignore, but check cautiously materials more than five years old. Because the youth world changes quickly, curriculum becomes outdated.) Review titles of all books in appropriate areas. Check filmstrips for possible resources.

(2) **Resource Center**—Many denominations provide area resource centers that are libraries of Christian education resources. If your denomination has one in your town or nearby, visit it to find out what it offers. Take home a catalog if possible. If there is a staff person on duty, enlist their aid in locating resources for your particular activities.

If your denomination does not have a nearby resource center, find out if other denominations do. Good youth resources often cross denominational lines. Most denominational resource centers will carry materials produced by several different denominations. In fact the collection of youth resources displayed in a Methodist center may be almost identical to the collections displayed in a Presbyterian or Episcopalian center. You will have to exercise caution mainly in the areas of sacraments and specific beliefs. A Baptist will not want to use Roman Catholic materials on baptism, but may find their materials on world hunger extremely useful.

To locate resource centers, start by asking your minister if she knows where one is. However, do not accept her word that there is none in your area as final. (Ministers are often unaware of such places.) So, if your minister cannot identify a center, ask a Director of Christian Education in a neighboring church of your denomination, or a staff person in the area (district, presbytery, association) office. If such questioning proves that your denomination does not have a resource center, ask friends who are members of other denominations or call churches of other denominations about their centers. In most metropolitan areas, this exercise will produce at least one center.

(3) **Church bookstores.** If you are lucky to have a good one in your area, check it out. Find the "youth section" but also ask a salesperson to point out other sections where you might find the kind of resources you need.

In using Christian bookstores it is wise to know the theological position of the management. Some are denominationally sponsored and therefore reflect the position of that denomination. Independently operated stores generally reflect the position of the owner. Therefore, it is useful to ask the owner or a salesperson to what church the owner belongs. Knowing this denominational background alerts you to materials you might want to evaluate with extra care.

(4) **Curriculum catalogs.** Most denominations or clusters of denominations produce catalogs of resources for Christian education. The resources include church school curriculum and a hodgepodge of other resources. More and more denominations are producing four to eight week mini-courses in booklet form on a vast variety of youth concerns. Such booklets can become basic resources for many youth group activities. To find such books when you need them, you or your church needs a small collection of these catalogs. Below is a list of several of these catalogs and addresses from which they can be ordered (usually free).

Christian Education: Shared Approaches Prospectus
    CE:SA is a curriculum system produced by twelve Protestant denominations. It includes four curriculums, each including some youth resources. You can use any of the resources you are not already using in church school. Materials especially useful to youth groups are: "Interpreting the Word" (grades 6, 7, 8) which includes three new biblical mini-courses each quarter, the "Youth Elect Series" of mini-courses in "Living the Word" and the mini-courses in "Doing the Word."

    Order from: any of twelve denominations including
               United Church Board for Homeland Ministries
               Division of Christian Education
               132 West 31st Street
               New York, NY 10001

Cokesbury Church and Church School Catalog
    This includes Methodist quarterly curriculum for church school classes and youth groups as well as several sets of youth elective courses.

    Order from: your local Cokesbury bookstore or
               Cokesbury
               201 Eighth Ave., S.
               P.O. Box 801
               Nashville, TN 37202

Fortress Press: Study Resources for Adults and Young Adults
    A booklet size catalog describes dozens of four to twelve week courses by Lutherans on study and worship concerns.

    Order from: Fortress Press
               Church Supply Stores
               2900 Queen Lane
               Philadelphia, PA 19129

Argus: Religious Education 1983
In addition to a large collection of posters, Argus offers a variety of study books and kits produced by the Roman Catholic Church.

Order from: Argus Communications
Dept. 50
P.O. Box 7000
One DLM Park
Allen, TX 75002

Winston Press: Christian Education Catalog
Winston offers the "Infinity Series" of youth mini-courses and several longer range youth study resources. Winston Press is a non-denominational religious education press affiliated with Holt, Rinehart, and Winston.

Order from: Winston Press
430 Oak Grove
Minneapolis, MN 55403

(5) **Resources in your community.** Your public library and any community colleges offer a wealth of resources on many subjects. To locate particular resources, ask organizations dedicated to that concern for help. For example, your local mental health department can provide free films, books, and even trained people to supplement programs about family life. If you have a Yokefellows chapter, they might be glad to introduce your youth to the local criminal justice system and their ministry to prisoners.

If you do not know your community well, find someone who does. Show your list of planned activities and ask him or her to point you to local resources related to specific activities.

There are probably more. However, this should provide all the resources you can possibly use. To identify your sources of resources, follow directions on page 44.

NAMING YOUR SOURCES OF RESOURCES

To make your own personal list of sources of youth ministry materials:

(1) Check your church library and curriculum closet. List the kinds of useful items you found and want to remember.

_____
_____
_____
_____
_____

(2) Write name, address, and phone number of any resource centers nearby.

_____
_____
_____
_____

(3) Write name, address, and phone number of useful church bookstores after you visit them to check them out.

_____
_____
_____
_____

(4) List curriculum catalogs you have ordered. (Store them in a safe place.)

_____
_____
_____

(5) Write name and phone number of persons who can identify local resources.

_____
_____
_____
_____

"WHAT MAKES A PROGRAM GOOD?"

Most of this section has dealt with how to select and prepare activities for a small youth group. The remaining question is "what makes a program good?" What is the difference in activities that are stimulating and those that fall flat? It is a question we all ask but which no one has answered definitively. However, there are a few ideas about what makes an activity good for a small youth group.

Good youth events consist of learning by doing. Five days a week, teen-agers sit at desks and study. There is a need for study in the Christian life—but it is usually done better in other settings. Youth groups are the settings for simulation games, mission projects, field trips, doing the work of the church, traveling, and playing together. A youth group involved in a good project may skip recreation without noticing it. If they are making posters for the CROP walk and want them up by next week, the task at hand is more satisfying than any game. A really good youth activity is seldom identified as "the program."

Many small youth groups often cannot risk deep sharing. Many youth resources suggest exercises that involve sharing important personal experiences and concerns. Most youth seek opportunities for such sharing. But it is a strange truth that such sharing requires a little distance. It is one thing to risk sharing personal thoughts with someone you see once a week at church or mainly at school. It is another thing entirely to risk sharing such thoughts with a brother, sister, or cousin. Therefore, most groups that include closely related youth have little interest or success with activities aimed at sharing and developing intimacy.

On the other hand, small groups that include youth who are not closely related can become very intimate sharing and caring cells. You have to know your group to know whether sharing is a good activity for it.

Three or four youth can enjoy and benefit from guests (although the guests will not be guest speakers) and occasional rented films. We generally consider such activities wasted on small groups. Adults are embarrassed to ask a person to meet with so few youth. We feel it is not worth $25 to rent a film for fewer than five viewers. But once again we are dealing with our attitudes. If four youth really want to learn about another branch of the Christian family, there should be no embarrassment in asking a leader of that church to meet with your four. Simply be honest in your invitation. Tell your intended guest how many youth will be involved as you explain the place, time, and subject. If your guest is willing, enjoy rather than apologize. In the same way, go ahead and rent the excellent film that directly relates to your current concern. The budget may not allow for many films but at even $7.00 per viewer, an occasional well-chosen film is a good activity.

Good youth activities often involve the youth in preparations. Such activities are seldom the result of youth working alone to plan and lead a program. But they do provide opportunities for youth to take specific responsibility. Thus a hayride set up by adults may be an "OK activity." But, if one youth arranges for the truck and hay, another calls all youth members to be sure they're invited and know they can bring a friend, and each young person brings a contribution to the food table—the hayride may become a "great activity." Successfully involving young people in such ways is more trouble for the adult leaders than doing the job themselves. Leaders have to check on how each young person is coming along with their job. That takes time. But that time can make a difference. When young people feel some ownership of what they are doing and are learning new skills and responsibilities, they are doing good activities.

This leads us to a final point: good programs are usually ones that the participants selected. An exploration of the occult will bore some groups and fascinate others. The best way to insure that a group's activities will interest a particular group is to involve that group in selecting their activities. Therefore, careful planning with youth is one of the best ways to offer good activities.

This has been a long answer to the original question "But what can we do with such a small youth group?" The summary answer is that you can do almost anything if you (1) define your purpose and direction, (2) select activities to carry out that purpose, and (3) have the resources that suggest both content and methods for exploring specific concerns and doing projects. Now that you can do these things, you are ready to ask questions about organization and leadership.

*WHAT WE CAN DO

WORSHIP

During Sunday morning service
  —Call to worship, scripture
  —Prayers, offering
  —Mini-dramas
  —Use of audio-visuals
  —Puppets
  —Music, musical
  —Instrumental music
  —Role play
  —Dance
  —Act out parable
  —Usher, acolyte
Regular attendance
Youth do entire service
Palm procession
Passover
Jewish Seder
Children's sermons
Design and lead worship service for children
Design and lead worship for vacation church school
Make banners

Outdoor worship
Easter Sunrise service
Youth choir
Conduct prayer service
Christmas program
Advent wreath lighting during worship service
Advent church school services (Fifteen minute service at beginning of church school for four Sundays in Advent)
Make chrismons for chrismon tree
Lenten services
Worship after football game
Worship at retreats or lock-ins
Lead worship for elderly
Design and lead early Sunday morning family service
Visit other churches
Handbell choir
Write on 3 X 5 cards thoughts or prayers for use in worship

Worship in catacombs (simulating early Christians)
Write hymns and songs (write words to familiar hymn or song tune)
Agape Meal/Agape Feast (a worship experience designed around a meal, after the Moravian tradition)
Worship workshop
Live nativity scene
New Year's Eve service
Clown ministry, Floyd Shaffer-style
Prayer at congregational functions
Hymn of the month (youth research and publish information in bulletin or newsletter)
Design and conduct worship at church picnic

STUDY

Church school curriculum topics
Other denominations
Worship
Social issues
Death
Death and dying (grief process)
Parent/youth relations
Other religions
Christian life-style at school
Life-style
—Simplicity
—Conservation
School
Hunger
Poverty
Environmental concerns
Christian living
Friendship
Prayer and meditation
Living the faith
The Ten Commandments
Beatitudes
Twenty-third Psalm
Apostles' Creed
Passover and Holy Week
Baptism and the Lord's Supper
Moses
Men of the Covenant—Old
   Testament
Value process
Values clarification
Identity
Relationships
Jobs as Christian vocations
Career exploraion
Making decisions
Handling conflict
Mark
Life and teachings of Jesus
Meaning of Jesus Christ
Bible quiz

People who encountered Jesus
Prepare mini-course for children
Bible study at coffee house
Bible study at retreat
Mini-course at retreat
Music
—Modern
—Church
—Hymns
—Christmas carols
Discussion of sermons
Science fiction
Study related to lectionary
Counseling center testing
Lenten studies
—Ash Wednesday
—Passion
—Good Friday
—Palm Sunday
—Easter
Eternal life and other options
The arts
Evangelism
Global concerns
Why poverty?
Spirituality
Confirmation/commissioning
Women of the Bible
Seasons of the church year
Denominational creeds
Field trips
Prophets
Prophecy
Paul
Puppetry workshop
Bible workshop
Intergenerational studies
—On honesty
—Communication
—Values
—Biblical

Communication workshop
Alternative celebrations
Love
Romans
Galatians
Who is God?
What is a Christian?
Denominational heritage
Denominational beliefs
Sex/sexuality
Dating
Marriage
Overview of the Bible
Alcohol
Drugs
Capital punishment
Criminal justice
Revelation
Weekly Bible study (outside of
   church school)
Caravan trip
Symbols
Movies
Visual arts
Youth problems
Commitment
Biblical simulations
Building a Christian community
Success
Our church's life
Community concerns
Prejudice/racism
Forgiveness
Students' rights
The occult
Parables
Stewardship
Violence
Censorship (TV, magazines,
   etc.)
Women's movement

MINISTRY WITHIN THE CONGREGATION

Help prepare church school
materials
Make visual aids for teachers
Team teaching in church school

Mothers'-Morning-Out during
Christmas vacation
Craft fair
Run A-V equipment

Mission fair (with meal of that
country)
Caroling (either to members'
homes or with adults)

MINISTRY WITHIN THE CONGREGATION—*continued*

Help with vacation Bible school
—Teaching
—Recreation
—Music
—Refreshments
—Nursery for VBS teachers
Serving in the nursery and extended session
Easter sunrise breakfast
Pancake breakfast
Buffet luncheon
Serve at church dinners
Restaurant for congregational dinner
Design mini-course for children
Lead Advent workshop for children
Church school substitute
Work with elderly and shut-ins
—Bake cookies and make containers out of oatmeal boxes
—Birthday cards, make gifts
—Make emergency telephone numbers book
—Adopt a grandma/pa
—Clean yards and odd jobs
—Run errands
—Take them shopping
—Telephone check-in
Tape ministry for shut-ins and hospitalized
Youth choir
Cantata with adult choir
Musicals
Dramas
Acolytes, ushers

Fun Night for family night dinner (youth lead all activities: recreation, group-building games, values exercises)
Catalog visual aids for church school
Youth visit youth (a welcome wagon for new youth)
New member assimilation (assign-a-youth)
Play piano or organ for accompaniment
Work with children's choir
Recreation and parties for children
Big brother/big sister for children (youth are big brother/sister to individual elementary children of the church)
Halloween party for children (spook house)
Serve on committees/task forces
—Evaluation committees
—Pulpit committees
Forum on leadership roles in the church
Intergenerational studies
Parent night/parent reception
Adult/youth seminars on topics
Adult/youth bowling teams, volleyball, softball
Serve ice cream at church dinner
Ice cream social (Mother's Day)
Carnivals

Design and prepare bulletin boards
Car wash
Yard work for members
Talent show
Bake and serve cookies between church school and church (with all youth present—emphasis on visibility)
Tutoring
Help with worship
Clean church yard
Slave Day, Rent-a-Senior
Live nativity
Easter egg hunt for children
Decorate church (Christmas)
Banners
Puppet show
—Have puppet workshop for youth—They then present show for children or for congregational dinner
Sponsor special food collection (collect from congregation for local needy families)
Present special programs or displays on study topics
Video presentation on church or church school, or on seasons of the church year
Interview adult classes (with or without tape recorder)
Do recreation at church picnic
Make posters for various emphases
—Christian education
—Youth ministry

SERVICE

Take care of lawns for elderly
—Rake leaves
Adopt a child (locally or overseas)
—Big Brother/Big Sister

Fast for CROP
CROP walk (CROP is the hunger program of Church World Service, Box 968, Elhart, Indiana 46514)

Urban camps
Teen center
Coffee house
Agency aides (Red Cross, Girls' Club)

SERVICE—*continued*

Neighborhood cleanup
City cleanup
Sponsor needy families
Toys for poor at Christmas
Give program for senior citizens
—Christmas
—Puppets
—Anytime
Craft projects to make gifts for elderly
Clown ministry
Brainstorm ongoing service to elderly
—Birthday cards
—Writing letter for them
—Singing
—Checking on (telephoning)
—Doing errands
—Taking them shopping

Help with Meals on Wheels
Parties or picnic for children's homes or retarded children's center
Singing for convalescent homes
Summer program for preschoolers in low-income neighborhood
Day camp in low-income neighborhood
Helping with Girls' or Boys' Club
Tutoring
UNICEF collection
Puppet shows for children
Help in library
—Saturday reading program
Shovel now

Work camps
Visits in day-care centers
Summer aiding in day care
Food and clothing collection and distribution
Recycling paper and aluminum cans
Education of community on social concerns by displays or presentation (connected to a study youth have done)
Help with city recreation program
Christmas for prisoners
—Make stockings and fill with toothbrushes, etc.
Invite non-church-related friends to activities

FELLOWSHIP

Retreats
Lock-ins (church-ins)
Movies
Eat (burger or pizza place)
Trips
Car caravans
Beach
Snow skiing
Water skiing
Talent show
Camping
Cold (rough) camping
Skating
Bicycling
Bowling
Caroling
Craft workshops
Craft projects
Refeshments in homes
Progressive dinners
Parties
—Halloween
—Valentine
Coffee house

Sports
—With other groups
—Baseball, softball
—Volleyball, soccer
—Basketball
Recreation (games)
Retreats with other church youth groups
Youth singing groups
Singing
Hayrides
Horseback riding
Swimming
Cookouts
Hikes
Square dance
Museums
Scavenger hunt
Polaroid scavenger hunt
Denominational youth conferences (synod, presbytery, district, association)
District camps

Youth rallies
Work camps
Community cultural events
Dances
Dance after football or basketball game
Jogging
TV viewing
Rafting
Canoe trips
Mimes
Carnival
Mission Fair
Crab soccer
Miniature golf
Ping pong
Pool
Trip to a college for a day
Rock concerts
Sailing
Values mini-course
Group-building activities
Cook dinner for parents
This Is Your Life

YOUTH MINISTRY: The New Team Approach by Ginny Ward Holderness. Copyright 1981 John Knox Press. Used by permission.

Patterns for Small Youth Fellowships

Even small youth fellowships come in many different shapes. They meet weekly, every other week, monthly, or occasionally. They have anywhere from one to eleven (yes eleven!) adult leaders. They meet at the church, in homes, or in community buildings. They include only senior highs, only junior highs, both senior highs and junior highs, or "all youth" (even a few grade school youth). Each group is unique.

But, among all these unique groups, one can detect several basic patterns that have been adapted to suit a particular situation. This section outlines several of these patterns. However, before examining these patterns, it is necessary to decide how many youth groups you want to form.

A PRELIMINARY DECISION: HOW MANY GROUPS WILL YOUR CHURCH SPONSOR?

Can one group include youth of a sufficiently broad age span? Or, would two or more groups be more effective? There is no one answer that is true for all churches.

The arguments for having only one youth group are strong. The principle argument is that the group will be larger (and one presumes "better"). There will be ten in one group instead of four or five youth in two separate groups, making more players for games, actors for plays, and workers for projects. The arguments for dividing church school classes may be less applicable to the activities of a youth group. Indeed, youth groups offer an opportunity for younger and older youth to know each other well. Older youth can tell younger ones truths they will not hear from an adult. Younger youth can offer older ones permission to play silly games without blowing their senior high cool. And last, but not least, one group requires fewer adult leaders than two or three groups. Anyone who has worked on enlisting adult advisors knows how much weight this argument carries.

The arguments for forming several youth groups are equally strong. The prime argument is that the interests, skills, and needs of older youth are significantly different from those of younger youth. Even in youth groups the best way to meet the needs of all may be to form at least two groups. The activities of each group can then be designed to meet the needs of that particular age. As a side benefit, youth get the stimulation of moving from one group and type of activity into another group and type of activity. Some people argue that without this change, youth become bored by the time they get to mid-high school. Youth activities seem repetitious to them. It is also argued that in a broad-aged youth group, the older youth dominate and lead while the younger youth are required to be followers. The younger youth are the losers here as they wait to gain the athletic strength, mental skill, and power to compete with the older youth.

Each church must make this decision by itself. There is no one right answer. Churches have succeeded and failed using single groups and several groups.

Once you know how many groups your church will sponsor, you are ready to look at the patterns.

The Standard Pattern

These groups of three or more youth meet weekly with two to four adult advisors. This can be called the standard pattern because it describes what we generally expect when we think of a youth group. The group meets weekly to pursue activities of study, worship, fellowship, and service. Meetings usually last from one to two hours on Sunday evenings or a set weekday evening.

The group's adult leadership generally includes two to four adults. One couple, or even one dedicated person, may serve as sole advisor(s), meeting with the group weekly and for special events. But, this is a big job for one. Even though they enjoy the work and form close friendships with the young people, many couples or individuals who undertake group leadership alone burn out. Some burn out within a year.

Others may last several years. But eventually most will cry, "enough!" Once solo advisors have burned out, it is hard to re-enlist them. They say, "We took our turn."

One way to lighten the load on advisors is to enlist two couples or four people for a group. The four work together. In some of these foursomes, all four attend meetings, knowing that the others can carry the ball when one or two are not there. One advisor going on vacation or getting sick does not close down the youth group. Other sets of advisors are held responsible for a specific activity or series of activities and generally attend only those activities for which they are responsible. However, all four will often work on and participate in major activities requiring extra adult leadership.

Having four advisors makes it possible to maintain continuity when adult leadership changes. Each year the church enlists two adult advisors to serve for two years. This provides a group with two experienced advisors and two new advisors each year. The combination provides both security and fresh ideas for both the adult leaders and the young people.

The main reason churches with small numbers of youth give for avoiding this standard pattern is that there are not enough youth to make it work. Adults question whether it is worth all the effort for three to five youth. Adults also wonder whether the youth would want to be part of such a small group.

Experience proves the fears are unfounded. Small groups can operate in the standard manner:

A church of one hundred fifty members regularly enlists four advisors to lead their active youth fellowship of six to ten (grades seventh-twelfth). The group meets from 6-7:30 every Sunday evening. They select mini-courses of study, go on retreats, present a Christmas play every year, pursue a variety of service projects, and are as close a Christian friendship group as can be imagined.

One rural church of thirty-seven members provides such a fellowship for three to six youth. The group at times includes children as young as fourth grade and others in high school. They meet each Sunday evening in the home of a member who provides a snack supper and a spacious den. Their minister (whom they share with another church) meets with them every other week, providing program leadership. When he is not there, the hostess advisor helps the group carry out activities planned by the minister and group the previous week.

Neither of these churches would hesitate to affirm the importance and value of their youth group. At times the first church has trouble enlisting youth advisors. But so does a big church enlisting larger numbers of advisors for their larger youth groups.

The young people in both of these churches do not consider their size a reason to fold. Most of them waited anxiously to age into the group, and have a high commitment to both the people and the activities involved.

So again, the key to making this pattern work is attitude. If three or more youth and a group of adults believe in it, any church can sponsor a weekly youth fellowship.

The Team Approach Pattern

The team approach is really an adaptation of the standard pattern. A group of three or more youth meet weekly to pursue study, worship, service, and fellowship activities. The distinctive characteristic of the pattern is that adult leadership is provided by a team of eleven adults. Two are enlisted as study advisors, two as worship advisors, two as ministry within the church advisors, two as service advisors, two as

fellowship advisors, and one as coordinator. All advisors meet with the youth to plan activities for the year. During the year each set of advisors works mainly on their assigned area but may come along as extra leadership on other events upon request.

At first glance this seems totally out of the question for small youth groups. (We're talking about more adult leaders than youth!) If your small group is sponsored by a small church, the team approach looks plainly impossible. (Eleven youth advisors? We can hardly find two!) But numerous churches are proving that it does work.

Cross Roads is a rural church of one hundred eighty members with a Senior High Fellowship of about eight and a Junior High Fellowship of three regular members. They have used this approach for both fellowships for one and a half years now. Since they combined ministry within the congregation and service, each group requires four pairs of advisors. Their two day a week DCE (that's me) serves as coordinator for both groups. That adds up to seventeen adults.

After working in this pattern for a year and a half, we have learned several things about its use with small youth groups:

(1) **The team approach does spread the load.** Each advisor is responsible for about eight sessions per year. Many who would never take on a full-time youth job, will tackle this more limited assignment. But—with decreased involvements come decreasing rewards. The adults do not have the opportunity to get close enough to the young people to reap the rewards of friendships and sharing that full-time advisors treasure. Consequently, advisors are easier to enlist at first, but some do not get enough out of their experience to motivate their doing it more than one year.

(2) **Adults can be recruited to work in their area of interest or skill.** The mission-oriented can take the lead in the service area while the adult who cannot imagine himself teaching organizes the fellowship activities. Adults can meet youth in an area where they have self-confidence. That makes enlistment easier, but youth get to know their adult friends in only one fairly narrow way. The fellowship advisors get tagged as party people because they are known only through parties. There is little opportunity to hear their views on youth issues or to pray with them. The pinch is tightest on the study advisors who often get tagged as serious sticks-in-the-mud. The official remedy is for advisors to join in as participants in some events they do not lead. But in very small groups, such participation easily results in having more adults than youth in attendance. That is awkward. Cross Roads' response to the study advisors' dilemma was to enlist the minister as study advisor. His relationships with the youth were broad and secure enough to surmount the "tagging."

(3) **Youth ministry becomes a more visible part of the congregation's life as more adults are involved.** More adults get to know the church's young people, at least a little bit. More adults feel personal

ownership of and take pride in the congregation's youth ministry. This effects policy decision, coffee hour conversations, and responses to occasional broken windows that result from exuberant recreation. But if the congregation is small, the pool of available adults is small. Consequently, the willing adults who are already wearing two or three hats at church must don yet another hat for the youth group. This can pose a problem. However, many willing adults prefer being a perennial member of a team to being full-time advisors for a year at a time. Each church must analyze its own situation.

(4) **More adults develop an awareness of and commitment to youth ministry, but they have to be trained.** Good advisors are not born; they are developed. It is often easier for two to four prople to build a common vision and get the training they need than it is for eight to ten people to do the same. What two people can hash through on the phone, ten people must call a meeting to do. The coordinator's job is crucial and challenging in this area. In many ways the coordinator must build and develop the advisor team just as the advisors build the youth group. The success of the advisors' team will determine the success of the youth group.

(5) **As indicated in the previous point, a strong coordinator is key.** Someone has to be around enough to know what is going on in the group. In addition to being trainer/advisor to the advisor team, the coordinator must make numerous phone calls to check on plans being made, keep calendar commitments clear, and generally be the oil that keeps the machine running. There is no "but" on this. The coordinator is key.

The team approach is described in great detail with step-by-step directions for its first year of use in *Youth Ministry: The New Team Approach* by Ginny Ward Holderness. Any church considering this pattern should purchase at least one copy of this book.

Cooperative Youth Group Patterns

Two or more churches can combine their youth to form cooperative youth groups. Such groups may supplement congregational groups or may take the place of such groups. There are several variations within the pattern:

Regular Cooperative Youth Events are special activities planned by two or more churches on a scheduled basis. They may occur monthly, quarterly, on fifth Sundays, or on any other schedule. The distinctive thing about such events is that they are attempts at meaningful activities that no one church could tackle alone. Films and guest leaders too expensive for one church are within reach when costs are shared. Simulation games and other learning activities that require large groups become possible when several churches combine their limited numbers of youth. The fun of large group games, the experience of singing with a large group, and the special sense of being part of a larger faith community all result from the scheduled events.

Such events may be scheduled into the activities of a weekly group or may stand alone in a church's youth ministry. It is quite possible that within a group of sponsoring churches, some would have weekly groups and others would not.

The planning group for such events needs to include at least one adult from each participating church, and may also include one youth from each church. In one case, the ministers from several churches work together informally as the planning committee. In a more structured planning group, the adult might be a youth group advisor or a person enlisted for this particular task.

Often planning groups plan a series of events (perhaps a year's worth) in order to have adequate time to invite guest leaders and order films. At this point, some planning committees assign responsibility for specific events so that few further meetings are needed. Other planning committees work together on all events—meeting more frequently.

Weekly Cooperative Youth Groups do the same kinds of things youth groups in a local congregation do. The distinctive thing is that the group is composed of youth from several churches. The churches combine financial resources and leadership to offer more youth ministry than they could offer alone.

One such youth group is a junior high group sponsored by seven small churches. Four of the seven churches sponsor Sunday evening youth groups, including broader age ranges. Three have no local youth group. On Wednesday afternoon young people are brought from the two area schools to the central church for an hour and a half of activities under the leadership of a DCE the churches hired as a group.

One fear about such groups is that they will decrease a young person's interest and participation in the local congregation. Experience indicates that this seldom happens. Care should be taken for the cooperative group to contribute to the congregations in service projects and such events as being the visiting choir. The group should also avoid scheduling activities that conflict with important congregational events. But youth ties to their congregation are usually quite strong. They see the cooperative events as extensions of the ministry of their own congregation and participate accordingly.

One-Time Cooperative Events and Trips are often a good introduction to cooperative youth ministry because they are one-time events. If you like it, you can plan more. If you do not like it, you can move on to something else.

These events often result from taking advantage of special opportunities. For example:

- Three churches ranging in size from one hundred eighty to five hundred and thirty-five combined efforts to sponsor a six-week-long summer program for junior high students. The group met on Wednesdays from 10:00 a.m. to 3:00 p.m. to produce the musical *Joseph's Amazing Technicolor Dreamcoat*, study the Joseph story, and have fun together. One church offered the services of their staff music leader. The prop and costume and recreation leaders were lay people from each of the churches. The ministers cooperated on the Bible study. The thirty junior high students involved had a very special summer experience no one church could have provided alone.

- A university town church of seven hundred that had very few youth around during the summer, and a neighboring church of one hundred forty members, once combined forces for a youth work week. Their job as a team of twelve youth was to repair an old school that was being used for senior citizen programs. During the week they were followed around by swarms of doting neighborhood children. These loving, bored children made such an impression that the group decided to finance, plan, and lead a week long day camp the following summer for those children. That was one cooperative event that naturally evolved into another.

- High School seniors and college students from seven churches went together on a ski trip the week after Christmas. Several of the ministers went along to ski and deepen relationships with young members who are often away from home.

Most of these events start with a person or a church with an idea or problem. The key to getting started is to hear such ideas or problems with a sense of openness. Some of the strangest, wildest ideas make the most useful realities.

Each of these patterns is a starting point, a design. They are like the patterns for sewing clothes. Two people can select the same pattern. But by the time each has selected fabric and buttons and changed this or that to suit their needs or whims, the final products are quite different.

These patterns for organizing youth groups are to be used in the same way. Let the fabric of your congregation determine their style. Adapt them to your particular needs and whims. The result will be a youth group that is a unique ministry of your congregation.

A WORD ABOUT WHERE MINISTERS FIT IN THE PATTERNS:

Congregations often look to their minister for leadership in youth ministry. Some ministers enjoy this ministry and train themselves to do it well.

Such interested ministers can be enlisted as advisors for youth groups. They may in rare cases be the only advisor. More often they will serve as part of a team of advisors. Ministers serving yoked fields can often serve on the team of each church, being present at each church in turn.

Interested ministers may serve as advisor to the advisors offering training, behind the scenes help in planning and resourcing, and generous doses of encouragement and support. A church using the team approach could enlist the minister as coordinator.

A minister who is not regularly present at youth meetings can be enlisted to lead activities for which she or he is particularly able. Ministers also enjoy invitations to participate in occasional activities as one of the group rather than as leader.

And it must be accepted that some ministers have little interest in or talent for youth ministry. That is OK too. These ministers can be great sidelines supporters. Everyone has their gifts.

The only role you dare not ask or allow your minister to assume is to be the only adult to whom youth relate and by whom youth feel loved. When the minister becomes the only adult friend and hero, youth ministry becomes a personality cult rather than a part of the congregation's life. Young people develop no real involvement in or commitment to the church. When the minister moves, the youth disappear into silence, somehow feeling that relating to the new minister or participating in new programs would be a betrayal of their lost friend.

The trick is to utilize each person—both layperson and clergy—to the fullest. The way to begin is with open, honest conversation. Discuss with your minister possible roles she or he might play in the youth group. Enlist ministers just as you do other youth leaders.

A good garment maker will tell you that the way to design clothes is to play around with different combinations of pattern and fabric until you create the desired garment. The same is true of creating a youth group. So take time to play around with the possibilities for your church. Below are some questions about the fabric and each pattern to stimulate your mental playing.

The Fabric

- Make a list of all the youth in your church.

- IF you formed one group:
  How many would be included?
  Who would be the leaders?
  What problems might you expect?

- IF you formed more than one group:
  Who would be in each group?
  How large would each group be during the next three years.
  What problems might you expect?

The Standard Pattern

- Make a list of people who might be willing to serve on a team(s) of four advisors.

- When and where might the group(s) meet?

The Team Approach

- Make a list of people who might serve in each area. Also make a list of potential coordinators.

- IN SMALLER CHURCHES: Would potential adult advisors in your church prefer to be full-time advisors for a year occasionally, or to be part of a larger team of advisors regularly?

- IN LARGER CHURCHES: Would it be possible to enlist teams of adults over year long terms and thus involve large numbers of adults over several years?

Cooperative Groups

- Brainstorm possible cooperative groupings in your area. Which churches would be interested in . . .

  —cooperation between churches of the same denomination?
  —cooperation between churches of different denominations?
  —cooperation between churches in a close geographical area?
  —cooperation between churches of the same size?

- Which kind of cooperative effort would be most appropriate to each grouping you created above?

  —regularly scheduled cooperative youth events?
  —weekly cooperative youth groups?
  —one-time cooperative youth events and trips?

On the Road

When we think of traveling with a group of youth, we tend to picture major productions requiring months of planning, buses, reservations, and significant amounts of money. But a small group can . . .

   . . . go in one car (or maybe two),

     . . . sleep on the floor at a friend's or relative's house,

       . . . stay at one camp site, and

         . . . get on the road with very little fuss.

For example, three teen-agers in one church had been after their minister to take them to King's Dominion (a theme amusement park several hours' drive from their homes). The Sunday before a two-day school vacation, they decided to go. They spent one day and evening at the park, slept in sleeping bags at the home of a seminary friend of their minister, toured the seminary the next morning to learn how ministers prepare for their work, and then drove home. The church paid for the gas. Each person paid for their own food and their admission to King's Dominion.

Longer trips involving more stops and greater distances take more planning, of course. But they are possible. In fact they are more possible for small groups than for large groups. Not only are trips possible, but they offer very special and unique opportunities for youth ministry. One congregation may choose to provide some time on the road as part of a youth fellowship or church school class. Another congregation for which weekly youth meetings are unworkable may plan for several trips a year as a specialized part of their ministry.

DESTINATION: TO MEET YOUTH NEEDS

Traveling with a church group can contribute to meeting almost every stated need of young people for Christian growth. Travel tends to create a close group where all can feel loved and supported. Four people in a car build warm friendships as they explore new places, hungrily search for a hamburger restaurant, and just visit as they drive. There are opportunities to really get to know each other and be better known. There are opportunities to take care of each other. There are also opportunities to get on each other's nerves. So, adults who want to meet individual needs for love must be alert to interpersonal problems and willing to work with the young people in solving them. Facing such problems directly and lovingly produces some tense moments, but it also contributes richly to growth of individuals and the sense of closeness, trust, and support youth need so much. The togetherness of traveling with a small group is therefore an ideal environment for meeting youthful needs for a loving, supporting group.

Travel gives youth a chance to form friendships with adult Christians they can know and emulate. Because the group is small and living close together, youth get a chance to really know the adult(s) who travel with them. As they play, work, and survive travel discomforts with this adult Christian, teen-agers form ideas about the kind of Christian they want to become and avoid becoming. Such ideas are part of the road map into their future.

Travel is the single most direct way to expose youth to the richness and diversity of the whole church. Instead of reading or seeing a film, young people can actually see and experience the church firsthand. The impact of such firsthand experiences is so very much greater than the impact of secondhand experiences that the effort and cost of travel is justified. Compare the world mission awareness of the teen who has studied missions and heard missionaries speak with that of a teen who has spent two weeks working with a missionary in Haiti. Or, watch thirteen-year-old Alice visit a presbytery meeting and recognize with surprise ministers whom she knew from church camp. "You mean they're part of Orange Presbytery, too? Neat!" Travel does make a difference!

Some kinds of travel enable youth to be the church today. Work camps can involve youth in mission work in this country and abroad. One or two youth can join youth from other churches in work camps sponsored by a group of churches or by a service organization. As few as four or five youth can plan and organize their own work camp serving the project of their choosing.

Travel can also encourage young people to ask questions, think, and search out the meaning of life. It may lead young people to see themselves more clearly as Christian. But, this happens more often as a fringe benefit or response to travel experience than as a result of our set intentions.

Travel, then, can meet many needs, but it cannot meet all needs. So, it is necessary to decide what needs we want to meet on any trip and to share that decision with everyone involved. Knowing where you're going and why is the beginning of a good trip.

TRAVEL SUGGESTIONS

(1) **The best youth trips I have been on or heard about include a variety of activities.** For example, the group that went to King's Dominion to play also stopped by the seminary to learn. At a work camp, five youth spent the morning and early afternoon restoring old houses in a poor community, then spent the late afternoon at the beach. Cooking dinner together during the evening completed their day. Another group spent days on the beach and evenings presenting puppet shows in nursing homes and a children's hospital.

This variety has numerous benefits. Most important is that each trip offers a more balanced experience of the Christian life. Therefore, (answering the cynic's point of view), young people don't show up at church just for the fun things. But also, (from the more positive point of view) young people are exposed more on each trip to the Christian life than to any one activity. This sets the tone for the group.

As a general rule, the worst trips are those that are purely for recreation. Frequently, relationships between adults and youth become a tug of war, with youth viewing adults as jailers placing limits on the one stated goal: to have a good time. Having broader goals can enable a group to bypass this disaster.

(2) **Be aware of the values you teach when you travel.** What you plan teaches. So, be careful when you decide . . .

—to spend the afternoon at a state park or an amusement park (enjoying God's creation versus energy consuming thrills).

—whether you will go to the "in" beach or a quieter one where the group will tend to play together more ("making the scene" versus building relationships).

—how much youth budget money can be spent on gasoline for a waterskiing retreat (price and style of recreation for God's people).

—will you eat out (and if so, where?), or will you fix your own meals (life-style for God's people)?

All of these decisions should reflect the best Christian life-styles and values because as youth travel together, they become a small Christian community. Adult leaders are responsible for helping young people form communities based on Christian values.

(3) **Share responsibilities for navigating, cooking, and cleaning up.** When working with a family-size group, it is easy for adult leaders to act like somewhat indulgent parents. This is exhausting for the adult and robs the youth of the chance to act as a responsible member of a group of peers. Instead, divide up the work. Do your fair share but organize things so that each young person also does theirs.

(4) **If you are cooking as a group, plan your menus in the car as you travel.** It takes up time and allows the group to plan for immediate meals rather than what we'll want two weeks from now.

(5) **A small youth group can become happily expert at The Shopping Blitz.** To prepare for the Blitz, a group literally tears up its shopping list. One person gets produce, another gets meat and dairy products, and so forth. One person, often the adult, gets the basket and checks out items as they are added. This approach gives everyone responsibility in group shopping and gets the job done quickly. (The Shopping Blitz was invented at 5:30 p.m. by seven hungry senior high skiers who wanted a spaghetti feast before the eight o'clock movie. They made it.)

Once you know why you are going and how you are going to get there, you're ready to begin dreaming about all the places you can go. The possibilities are exciting and almost endless. Browse through the travel catalog on the following pages. Imagine the youth of your church on each trip. How would they travel? Where would they stay? What would they gain from the experience? Try combining several of the suggestions into one trip.

One of the most difficult parts of traveling with youth for the first time is convincing the young people and yourselves that travel is really possible. A group may need to talk about traveling first. In planning, groups need to zanily suggest they visit Zaire on spring vacation or go backpacking on Mt. Everest. After getting giddy picturing yourselves assaulting Everest, you may believe that you could explore a natural wonder six hundred miles away. So dream, laugh, and talk for a while. Then, be ready to travel when the opportunity presents itself.

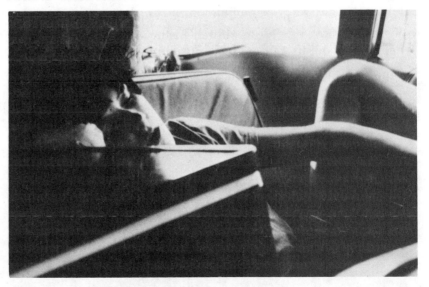

TRAVEL CATALOG

● Visit an official body of your denomination in session. Learn how it works and meet the people who make it work.

● Tour the headquarters of your denomination.

- Swap visits with the youth of a church very different from your own. Some match-ups to consider:
  - —two churches of different ethnic backgrounds
  - —a city church and a rural church
  - —an old church and a new church
  - —a big church and a small church
- As a group, attend a camp or conference sponsored by your denomination. (Some conference centers have cottages where groups can live and cook their own meals while attending a conference.)
- Visit a church-sponsored mission project in this country or abroad.
- Visit church-sponsored college(s). Stay a night on campus and talk to both students and the chaplain about college life.
- Take a show "on the road." Puppet shows, singing groups, skits or plays can often be scheduled in churches, hospitals, nursing homes, and other institutions.
- Camp, focusing on building group relationships and enjoying each other (where you go is not critical).
- Camp, focusing on exploring a wonderful part of God's world with attention to our role in that world.
- Camp, living cheaply as you get where you want to go.
- Backpacking trips offer everything that camping does for the more athletic and adventuresome. Backpacking requires an experienced leader.
- River rafting is offered in many areas by companies that provide equipment and guides for reasonable fees.
- Canoeing trips of one day to a week build a community of fellowship and provide opportunity to enjoy the natural world.
- Sailing is more difficult than rafting or canoeing, but some groups master it and go sailing together.
- Work camps are sponsored by many denominations and service groups. Check with your area office to find out what your denomination offers.
- Visit tour sites related to church history. Look for places that offer demonstrations and plays and hands-on exhibits rather than museums.
- Combine several of the above to explore one city. Example: A Connecticut group visiting New York City stayed in a church in Greenwich Village, toured St. John the Divine cathedral, saw the musical *Godspell,* drove through some of Harlem, and met some youth who lived in the city.

Recreation

Recreation is often seen as almost a bribe in youth ministry. It is the reward for doing what the adults really want the youth to do. "As soon as we finish this program, we can play," we say, trying to refocus youth attention on the task at hand.

Recreation is sometimes seen as seasoning or spice for youth ministry. Playing together makes doing the real youth ministry more palatable. "Since that class party, our attendance is better and relationships are smoother."

But recreation *is* youth ministry. Recreation meets needs and provides opportunities unavailable in any other form of youth ministry. As they play together, young people and their adult leaders can develop a very special community where young people can love and feel loved. All players feel accepted as they are in recreation at its best. As adults and youth play together, they become almost peers. Therefore, they become more open and accessible to each other. Hero friendships deepen. As they play together, youth (particularly younger teens) learn Christian attitudes toward competition. In our very competitive society, there are few other places they will encounter these attitudes. (Note: These sentences begin with the phrase "as adults and youth play *together*" because many opportunities for ministry are lost if the youth play while adults watch or referee. So even if you are not needed to make up a team—play. The silliness and even the aching muscles are part of the price we pay for ministry. Playing can also be fun!)

Books have been written about the importance and function of recreation in youth ministry, and this book is not the place to detail this broad subject. Instead, we will start from the assumption that recreation by itself meets some of the needs of youth and therefore has an important place in youth ministry.

Recreation can be provided in many settings. Even a small number of youth may be enough to form a sports team for play in a church league. Much depends on the rules of the league. Some leagues are very specific about a player's church membership and age. Small groups have trouble making it in such leagues. But many other leagues are more loosely defined—accepting almost any team a church or group of churches can field. In such a league, small groups have a chance. For example, one ninety-member church with fewer than ten active youth regularly fields a team in the Young Woman's Church Softball League. The team varies from game to game but generally includes women from about thirteen years old to some in their early twenties. The fellowship of this team is for some youth their only contact with the church. But during that contact they form friendships, enjoy a close relationship with some adult Christian heroes, and experience the love of a Christian community. With dividends like those, we cannot afford to dismiss too easily the possibility of sponsoring youth sports teams.

Parties or similar one-time events are another form of recreation. Two or more can enjoy their Christian fellowship doing almost any activity from the "Fellowship" part of the "What We Can Do" list on page 49. Doing something together, such as bowling or cooking a meal, is often the most successful recreation for small groups. Indeed small groups can do things together a large group cannot! For example, a kite party where junior high students make and fly their own kites would be all but unmanageable with twenty—but is a treat with four.

For parties that require larger numbers, enlarge your group by encouraging everyone to invite a friend or inviting one or more other groups to join you. When just four each invite a friend, the group becomes just big enough for "party games." When two or three churches combine their youth, there are enough people and money to rent the skating rink or have a "swim and gym" party at the Y.

But the recreation that produces the richest results is time spent playing together as a part of regular group meetings. Playing with a group that you also study, worship, and serve with deepens the meaning of all that you do together. Almost all successful youth groups play together regularly. Unfortunately, this kind of regular recreation is often the most challenging to provide. Advisors worry about finding enough good games to keep a small group active on a regular basis. And it is hard. Many games like volleyball, softball, and even kickball require more players than a small group can provide. But there is one helpful fact.

Youth enjoy some games the way children (of all ages) enjoy some stories. There is great pleasure in playing a certain game or hearing a favorite story again and again. A youth group can develop a repertory of favorite games from which they choose each week. That repertory will change slowly over the years as one at a time, games fall into disuse and new games are added. A group's repertory may not be very large. Five games offering a variety of active and quiet play can be plenty.

The adult leaders need to be aware of what is in the repertory, which games are waning and which games are strong. Instead of providing new games for every meeting, adult leaders stay on the lookout for occasional new games to introduce as needed. Youth may also introduce new games from time to time. Some games will fall flat—some will be enjoyed once, and a few will work their way into the group's collection.

It is hard to say exactly why a game makes it into a group's repertory. Of course, the basic qualification is replayability. Many party games and stunt games can only be played once and must be saved for one-time events. Strategy games and athletic games, which require no special prowess, are replayable. Competition can be fun if it matches players fairly evenly and the focus is on the playing, not the score. Therefore games based on a skill all share and those where there is frequent reversal of winners and losers are good choices. Other games are successful because they meet a need. For example, *Sardines* a perennial junior high favorite, seems to satisfy the need of younger teens to be part of the "in group." There is something delightful about being crammed into a dark closet trying to stifle the giggles that could give away your location. And if you are an outsider during one round, you will probably be an insider during the next. Finally, it must be noted that a game quickly earning a place in one group's repertory will fall flat in another group. So, a playful sense of trial and error is in order.

The best source for replayable games is the recreation shelf at your public library. On these shelves you can generally find several large books containing directions for group games. Though they may claim to be children's games, most of them work well with youth. One of my favorites is *The World Book of Children's Games* by Arnold Arnold (New York: World Publishing, 1972).

Use the game directions in these books as starting points from which you and the group begin to create games that particularly suit your desires. For example, *Cup Over* is an adaptation of a game that called for bowling pins. At first we substituted old milk cartons but later found paper cups worked and were easier to use. A group can also change rules, boundaries, and team arrangements to produce a more interesting, playable game. At times—tinkering with a game is as much fun as playing it.

The remainder of this chapter is a collection of games that have been part of the repertory of several small youth groups. They are generally arranged from the more active to the quieter games.

CUP OVER can be played with two, but is better with four or more players divided into two teams. The playing area (either outdoors or a large play room) is divided in half. Each team arranges five paper cups in an area drawn off in the same part of each court half. Teams remain in their own half of the court as a ball is kicked back and forth. The goal of each team is to knock their opponents' cups over or out of the drawn-off target area while protecting their own cups. To begin play, the ball is set on the floor at the mid-line. One player from each team puts a foot on the ball and at the signal, tries to kick the ball into her own territory. Players cannot touch the ball with their hands, except to protect themselves. When any player kicks the ball so that it gets above waist-high, the opposing team gets one free kick with the offending team off the field.

The game requires an alert, strong-willed referee to call above the waist shots and declare free shots. As a group is learning the game, it is best for an adult to referee. But as the referee's role is understood, gracious treatment of referees is ensured if youth takes turns in this role.

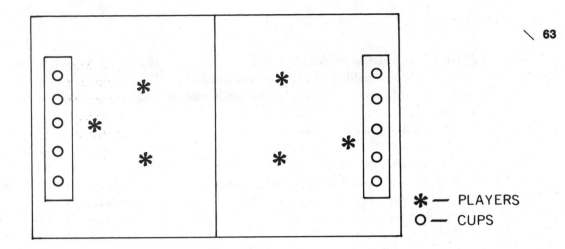

* — PLAYERS
○ — CUPS

(NOTE: The easiest way to mark boundaries on a floor is to use masking tape, which can be left on the floor of a multi-purpose room indefinitely. However, after several months it is difficult to peel up. To avoid this in rooms that must sometimes be tape-free, replace the tape regularly.)

SARDINES is hide-and-seek in reverse. One person hides while all other players count to one hundred. (Counting becomes a game in itself when orchestrated by a conductor who directs the group to count softly or loudly, smoothly or jumpily. Solo parts can be alternated with total group choruses.) Players then spread out searching for the hider. A player finding the hider quietly joins him or her in the hiding place. A clever seeker who finds the hider when other seekers are around will move on and then return to join the hider alone. Soon hiders are packed into their corner "like a bunch of sardines" trying not to giggle as they listen to the decreasing number of seekers wondering where everyone went. When the last seeker finds the hider, begin another round. You may decide that the first finder or the last finder will be the next hider, or you may take turns.

Sardines can be played anywhere—indoors or out. Clear boundaries are essential. Bathrooms, the janitor's closet, the sanctuary, the room where the baby is sleeping, the bed of prize rose bushes, and other such places must be formally declared either in or out-of-bounds.

Older youth can enjoy playing sardines in a small church building or home in the dark. Younger youth seldom have the self-control to avoid getting hurt or breaking something when playing in the dark. They prefer to run through a fairly safe playing area as they search.

PERSECUTION was invented by four junior high students after a program where they reenacted some life situations of persecuted early Christians. It resembles many other games. In fact you may know an identical game under a different name.

One player is selected as the soldier and given a can of pebbles to rattle or a bell to ring as he walks. All other players are Christians. The playing area is determined. It may include the whole church or house or it may be played in a defined area outside (this game is not advised for a house full of valuable antiques). Let everyone know about areas that may be out-of-bounds. The soldier goes to his base (preferably a closet or small room where the door can be closed) and counts to two hundred. While he counts, the Christians find a place to hide together and select a meeting place. The soldier then begins walking his duty, rattling his noisemaker (like clanking armor) as he moves. Christians each try to get to the meeting place without being tagged by the soldier and sent to the Coliseum for the rest of the round. Christians may move individually or in a group.

The key to this game is playing in an area that offers enough options for the Christians but not so many that the soldier's job is impossible. One floor of a church building is usually delightful. A two-story playing area is too frustrating for the soldier.

FOURSQUARE is one of those games that is played by a slightly different set of rules in every neighborhood. Players stand inside larger squares or outside smaller squares. They may or may not allow the ball to be returned to the previous player. (The following description is based on the current rules of one particular church.)

On the floor or ground, mark off a square about ten feet long on each side. Divide that square into four equal squares (five feet on a side). Number the squares from one to four around the larger square. Square one is the highest. Square four is the lowest and the square into which new players enter.

One player stands in each square facing center. The player in square one is the server. She bounces the ball in her own square, then hits it into another square. Whenever a ball bounces into his square, a player must hit it into another player's square before it bounces again. He may not return it to the player who hit it to him. Balls that hit the line are replayed. As they play, players may step outside of their own square but may not step in another player's square. When a player misses a ball or fails to hit it into another square, play stops while she leaves the court and all others move up a square. If only four are playing, the offending player moves to square four and the others move up a square. If there are more than four players, a line forms by square four. Offending players go to the end of the line and wait until they again take a place in square four and rejoin the play.

With four players, the players make joint calls about whether a ball was on the line or out-of-bounds and which player is out. When there are five or more players, the first person in the line serves as referee while waiting her turn.

PING-PONG and **BADMINTON** are active games for two or four players played with purchased equipment. They can be adapted for more than four players by using the foursquare model of rotation. One position is designated as entry position. Any time a player fails to return a ball, he goes to the end of the waiting line; all players below him move up one position; and the first player in line takes the bottom position. Score may be kept as in a regular game. Or the game may simply be played for the fun of the volley.

MARBLES games, which were once played everywhere, are unknown in some areas. Many game books include a chapter on marbles games, and there are even whole books of marbles games. Marbles can be played indoors or outdoors. The only equipment required is a sack of marbles and something with which to draw a ring on the ground or floor. Did you know there are official national marbles tournaments?

Other Active Recreation for Small Groups:

> *TENNIS*
> *POOL (BILLIARDS)*
> *TETHERBALL*
> *FRISBEE* games (try adapting any ball game for play with frisbees)

THE FLOUR GAME can be played with two or more players. Spread a sheet of newspaper on the floor. Completely pack a paper cup or glass with flour. Turn the cup over on the newspaper and gently slide the cup up until the cup-shaped tower of flour is standing. (This takes a little practice. The only secret seems to be firmly packing the flour and overfilling the cup so that the flour is slightly rounded above the lip of the cup.) Stand a dime on its edge at the center of the top of the flour tower. Players sit on the floor, taking care not to move the newspaper.

The first player uses a table knife to take a slice off a side of the tower, then passes the knife to the next player. Each player in turn must make one complete cut from the top to the base of the tower. The slice may take almost half of the tower or it may just shave one side. Play continues until a player collapses the tower. That player must push the dime out of the flour using her nose or teeth. (If youth are unwilling to play if they risk getting flour on their face or hair, omit this step.) The cup is then repacked and another suspenseful round begins. As groups become expert, they discover endless tricky cuts and find that a dime can be supported by an incredibly thin column of flour.

CAUTION: Flour on the face is funny. Flour in the eyes hurts. So, warn players before they nose in after that dime. Players who wear glasses have a definite advantage here.

SET BACK is a card game for two to seven players. It requires more strategy than luck. The dealer deals six cards to each player. Beginning with the player to the dealer's left, each player bids from one to four indicating the number of points they intend to make if allowed to name trump. Players may pass. To enter a bid a player must increase any other bid already made by at least one point. Bidding stops when a bid of four is reached, or when every player has had an opportunity to bid, whichever comes first.

The highest bidder wins the right to declare trump by leading a trump as the first card of the first trick. As on all tricks, all players must follow suit if possible. If a player cannot follow suit, she plays a card of another suit. Any trick is taken by (1) the highest trump, or (2) the highest card of the same suit as the first card played in that trick. The player who wins a trick wins the right to lead the first card of the next trick.

For each hand, one point is given the player who takes the highest trump, one point is given the player who takes the lowest trump, one point is given the player who takes the Jack of trumps, and one point is given the player who scores "game." Each player computes their game by adding point values of cards in tricks they have taken (10's count 10; Aces, four; Kings, three; Queen of hearts, diamonds, and clubs, two; Jacks, one; and the Queen of spades, minus thirteen). The player with the highest game score wins one point for the hand. If the high bidder who named trump for the hand does not make his bid, he is set back the amount he bid. If he is set back more points than he has, he goes in the hole computing a negative score.

To begin the next hand, move the deal to the immediate left of the previous dealer. The game's goal is to accumulate a pre-set score, usually between seven and ten.

I DOUBT IT can be played as a freewheeling game of chance, or as an exercise for the quick-witted who can remember who played what. Either way, it is fun.

All the cards of a standard deck are dealt to the three or more players. Any cards remaining after the last complete deal are put in the center face down to start the discard pile. The player to the dealer's left begins by laying from one to four cards face down on the discard pile saying "This is _____ (state number) twos." The player to her left then lays from one to four cards face down on the discard pile saying "This is _____ (state number) threes." The next player plays fours and so on. After aces are played, the process is repeated as the next player plays twos. The goal is to be the first player to discard his or her entire hand.

This is one game in which the truth is not required. Indeed, no matter what he has in his hand, a player must discard from one to four cards claiming they are the required kind of card. However, if another player says, "I doubt it" before the next person plays, the player must prove he told the truth or pick up the entire discard pile. If the player proves his innocence, the challenger must pick up the discard pile.

SPOONS requires three players but is more fun with five or more. In the middle of the table spread out one fewer spoons than there are players. Then deal each player four cards. The remaining cards are placed beside the dealer. The dealer begins play by drawing the top card on the pile and deciding either to pass it on to the next player or keep it, passing another card from his hand to the next player. The goal of each player is to accumulate four cards of the same number value (for example: four queens or four threes). Reaching that goal is the basis on which players decide what cards to keep and what to pass. As soon as the dealer has passed a card to the next player, he draws another card and repeats the process. The faster the play is, the better. Soon every player is frantically picking up and passing cards. If the dealer's stack is used completely, the dealer keeps play going by drawing cards from the discard pile of the last player in the circle. When a player has four cards of the same number she reaches for a spoon. Some groups insist that this move be accompanied by the cry, "Spoons!" Others allow a player to be as open or stealthy as she wishes. In either group as soon as one spoon is taken, all other players reach for one of the remaining spoons. The player who is left without a spoon becomes the next dealer.

BACK ALLEY can be played with more than eight players but is at its best with four to six players. It involves both quick thinking and luck. The number of cards dealt changes in each hand. In the first hand, cards are distributed equally up to a maximum of thirteen cards (when four are playing distribute a maximum of twelve cards). In each following hand, one card less than the preceeding hand of cards is dealt until only one card is dealt to each player. In hands following that, one more card is dealt to each player than was dealt in the previous hand until the maximum hand is again dealt.

After cards are dealt, extra cards are laid face down on the table. The top card is turned to determine trump. All players, beginning with the player to the dealer's left, get one bid to declare the number of tricks they intend to take. Any player may make any bid from zero up to the number of cards dealt for that hand. The total number bid by all players together may be less than or greater than, but not equal to, the number of cards dealt for that hand. The last bidder is therefore required to set her bid so that the total of all player's bids does not equal the number of cards dealt. This insures, often at the last bidder's expense, that not all players can be successful in attaining their bid.

The highest bidder (if more than one player make the same high bid, the *first* player to make that bid is the high bidder) opens play by leading the first card of the first trick. Other players, playing in clockwise order, add one card to the trick. Players must follow suit if possible. If they cannot follow suit, they may play a trump or play a card of some other suit. The trick is taken (1) by the highest trump played, or (2) by the highest card of the suit led. The player who takes the trick lays it face down in front of him. He then leads the next trick. Play continues until all cards have been played.

Each player who makes *exactly* what he bid scores twenty points plus the number bid. Thus a player making his three bid scores twenty-three points, and a player who bid zero and takes no tricks at all scores twenty points. A player who takes *more* tricks than she bid gets only one point for each trick taken. Thus a player who bid two but took four tricks scores four points. The unfortunate player who takes *less* than the number of tricks he bid scores *minus* twenty as well as *minus* one point for each trick taken. Thus a player bidding three but making only 1 scores minus twenty-one. Each hand's score is added to each player's previous score.

The game may be declared to be accomplished after the one card hand, after dealing has gone from maximum to one and back to maximum again, or when a player achieves a pre-set score. During play the deal moves to the immediate left of the previous dealer for each new hand.

Other Familiar Card Games Youth Enjoy:

> **HEARTS**
> **BLACK JACK (TWENTY-ONE)**
> **CRAZY EIGHTS**
> **RUMMY**
> **UNO** (played with a special deck of cards, available in games stores and many department stores)

Purchased Games for Small Groups of Youth:

Many of us have purchased games that small numbers of youth can enjoy together. As a general rule, games with brisk play and limited length are most enjoyable. Word games such as Scrabble favor the academically talented and can get bogged down. A long game such as Monopoly is only successful on those rare and wonderful times when a group spontaneously decides to devote an evening to it.

Below is a list of purchased games that have proven fun in small groups. The list is by no means complete. Add others you have played. Take a trip to a toy and game store just to browse. You may rediscover some wonderful game you haven't played in years and/or find some new useful games.

TWISTER

AGGRAVATION (This comes in a two-four players and a two-six players size. The larger one with five or six playing is a faster paced, more hilarious game)

YAHTZEE

PICK-UP STICKS

CHINESE CHECKERS

DOMINOES

TIDDLYWINKS

CLUE

CHAPTER 4

CONFIRMATION

One of the needs of youth identified in chapter 1 is the need for young people to see themselves as Christians. After a childhood of learning their way into the Christian community and learning about the faith of that community, teen-agers are in a position to make decisions about what they believe and how that will shape their lives. Just as Jesus challenged his disciples with the question, "But who do you say that I am?" a church must stand back to challenge each young person, "You have heard and seen and experienced what we believe, now what do you believe?" This challenging can be part of the ongoing youth ministry of a congregation. However, many churches focus on this need in a special rite, often preceded by a program of study. This may be called confirmation, commissioning, communicant's class, or just "joining the church." (In this chapter I will use the term "confirmation.")

At its least effective, confirmation is a special worship service that probably rates some new clothes. Teens are required to attend from one to six of the minister's lectures, which will probably rate higher on pranks and boredom than comprehension. After the ritual of confirmation, teens are able to vote at church meetings and can be elected to office but probably will not be. In some churches, confirmation entitles youth to graduate from church school.

But confirmation can be a very meaningful and challenging time for both young people and their congregations. It becomes so when confirmation is understood not as a rite to be performed or a program to be done but as a decision to be made and celebrated. The focus is on the individual. All programs and rites are planned to help that individual face and make the decision of personal commitment.

Approaching confirmation in this way changes the questions a church asks about providing confirmation. Instead of wondering whether we have enough for a class or how many meetings are necessary or where we can get materials for those meetings, we ask what activities would help young people make intelligent, careful decisions.

To answer that question, we must look closely at the decision we are placing before the young people. In most congregations, confirmation includes two related decisions. The first and foundational one is the faith decision about the personal lordship of Christ. The second is the decision to live out part of the relationship with Christ as a member of a particular congregation. To make these decision, a person must:

(1) understand what a church is and does.

(2) know and appreciate the congregation's way of worship.

(3) understand the role and significance of sacraments.

(4) know how the church is governed.

(5) understand the basics of the church's faith.

Obviously, no short-term program can provide all of this. For most youth this knowledge and understanding will have been forming as they participated in the church during childhood. What is needed at confirmation time is a thorough summarizing and clarifying of what they already know. Pieces of information gathered here and there need to be knit together into a related whole. Questions of clarification need answering. Childhood conceptions need sharpening. And childhood misconceptions need straightening out.

Understood this way, confirmation preparation becomes less a special class and more a period of intense and reflective involvement in the Christian life. When a young person is ready, it is the congregation's task to provide a plan for that period. The plan at its best includes a variety of activities. Participation in specific parts of the congregation's work and worship may be required. Reading can be assigned. Special projects may be carried out.

Most denominations produce a plan for this period in the form of a study book with a leader's guide. The quality of these books varies. But because of their format, people tend to use them to create scholastic courses. There are other possibilities.

CREATING YOUR OWN CONFIRMATION PLAN . . .

The remainder of this chapter is a kit to create a confirmation plan tailor-made for the needs and abilities of a particular young person or group. The kit is reuseable. It can be added to as you find new resources or create new learning activites. There are six sections in the kit. Each of the first five is related to one of the five kinds of understanding or knowledge a person needs in order to make a meaningful confirmation decision. These five sections are titled "Tasks." Each of these "Task" sections briefly describes the topic and lists several activities that enable young people to clarify and build on their understanding in that part of the Christian experience. The sixth section lists activities that help youth make their own decision based on the learnings gained from the five confirmation "Tasks." This section is titled "Making the Decision" and suggests ways the youth who choose confirmation can prepare for the ritual.

To create your program, select one or more activities from each of the sections. Arrange brief descriptions of the chosen activities on one page as a check-off sheet for each young person. List every expectation and be specific. If you require regular worship attendance, list the dates of worship during the confirmation period with space for checking services attended.

. . . FOR A GROUP

In preparing a record sheet for a small group, you may want to provide some choices that allow for personal preferences. For example, each young person might be asked to participate in two mission activities chosen from a list of six.

At an opening meeting with youth and their parents, the worksheet becomes an outline of the program. Go through the sheet explaining each activity, pointing out special dates, alerting youth to activities offering them choices, and answering questions. This process usually whets everyone's enthusiasm for the work ahead and helps both parents and youth grasp the purpose and meaning of confirmation. Youth realize that confirmation is something they will do, rather than something that will be done to them. And the support of parents in helping youth keep up with dates of special events is secured. At the end of this meeting, each young person takes his own record sheet. He records his work to present to the congregation as a sign of the care with which he has prepared for the confirmation decision.

The Sample Record Sheet was created for four junior high students in a Presbyterian church. Many of the tasks required individual work and participation in the ongoing life of the church. For example, they were required to participate in a course on the Sermon on the Mount already scheduled for youth church school classes. (Most of them were regular church school attenders, so this was no added job.) The group also met with the minister six times to study together. Their work was done over a three month period.

. . . FOR ONE PERSON

Because it is focused on a personal decision, confirmation is by nature more individual than group oriented. So, once again we who minister to small numbers of youth are the fortunate ones. We have the possibility of challenging each young person with the confirmation decision on a one-to-one basis when they are personally ready.

The confirmation worksheet offers one straightforward way to plan for and carry out confirmation on an individual basis. The minister or adult advisor may select appropriate activities and arrange them on a record sheet for a particular young person. However, some youth (especially older youth) can both enjoy and benefit from working with their adult advisor in selecting activities that will make up their program. In this process a young person gains understanding of the purpose of his or her work, chooses the most appealing activities, and begins taking responsibility for her confirmation program and decision.

The record sheet activities involve youth in activities with a variety of groups and individuals. But there are also a number of study activities. All of the activities described in each section can be done by one youth working with one adult. Two can study creeds and scripture, plan worship services, view and discuss filmstrips, and explore hymns together. One-on-one study and discussions offer opportunities for in depth exploration of personal faith and Christian living that are not available in larger groups. Indeed, people who have had the privilege of such an individual confirmation experience often point to it as one of the most meaningful times in their Christian lives.

One Fear (and an Assurance)

At first glance a confirmation record sheet promises a lot of work. (Some young people and parents may say "too much work.") It *is* work. The decision is faced carefully and seriously. After the program, however, students, parents, and the congregation are justifiably proud. Confirmation becomes a very special event for everyone. Completing it gives young people a new sense of their identity and worth as part of Christ's body. The consensus is that the results are worth the work. And if the work is spread over several months, the job is not too demanding for either youth or adults.

One Potential Problem (and a Solution)

Ministers are generally expected to take charge of confirmation programs. However, many small churches do not have a full-time minister. It is also a fact that ministers differ in their ability to work and communicate effectively with teen-agers. Therefore, a minister might want to organize a confirmation program in which another adult leader in the congregation serves as primary advisor with a young person. The minister's job is to provide the adult with resources needed and to check in with each youth-adult pair occasionally to learn what progress is being made. When care is taken in matching adult leader and young person, a warm friendship and amazing growth in faith may be reported by both.

SAMPLE

CONFIRMATION RECORD

Full Name _____ Telephone _____

In preparation for confirmation, you will need to do each of the following below. (Use this folder to keep records of what you have done. Bring this with you to each confirmation meeting.)

1. Attend all confirmation class meetings:

  —Tonight's meeting with parents

  —What is the church?

  —How does the church do its work?

  —Worship and sacraments

  —Discuss the Gospel of Mark

  —Prepare statements of faith

  —Share statements and plan confirmation worship service

Foldline

8. Choose one of the following ways to tell what you believe about God, Jesus, the church, and being a Christian. You will be asked to share this with the Session as part of your examination for membership.

  write your own creed

  write an essay

  write a song or poem

  put together some pictures or slides as a collage or slide show

  check any other idea with Steve

9. Be examined by the Session on May 23 (7:30 p.m.).

10. Those who decide to make their confirmation promises and are accepted by the Session will be confirmed on Pentecost Sunday (May 30) during the morning worship service.

2. Attend the church school course on the Sermon on the Mount. Check each week you attend.

March 14 ———   April 4 ———
21 ———   11 ———
28 ———   18 ———

3. Attend worship regularly and fill in at least two Worship-sheets, and the Sermonsheet for April 18. Check below the Sundays on which you attend worship. Add a star to the Sundays for which you do the Worshipsheets. Save all sheets in your folder.

March 14 ———   May 2 ———
21 ———   9 ———
28 ———   16 ———
April 4 ———   23 ———
11 ———
*18 ———
25 ———
(Sermonsheet will be provided)

4. Read the Gospel of Mark before _____. As you read make a list of the important things Jesus did. When you finish Mark, choose the ten most important things Jesus did. Bring your list to class.

—— foldline ——

5. Read the Bible and pray everyday using The Mustard Seed or some other guide you checked out with Steve.

6. Attend the first half-hour of the Session meeting on March 28 at 7:30 p.m. (If you miss this, attend the first half-hour of the meeting on April 25.)

7. Carry out and report to the class at least two of the following parts of the work of the church:

—— pack clothes for shipping to missions.

—— work on cemetery clean-up day.

—— ride with one of the Cross Roads Meals-On-Wheels deliveries (the week of Easter vacation).

—— go visiting with the pastor or a ruling elder.

—— visit the Presbyterian Home in High Point and prepare a way to tell the congregation about it before the May offering for the home.

—— read the material about "The One Great Hour of Sharing" to plan either a poster or announcement to the congregation before Easter.

—— read Love in the Mortar Joints (a book about church people who are building homes for people who need them).

—— read a biography of a Christian leader (check with Steve).

—— any other project you want to do for the church (check with Steve).

TASK #1

UNDERSTAND WHAT A CHURCH IS AND DOES

Before joining an organization, potential members expect to know the group's purpose and goals. Potential church members need a clear picture of the purpose and goals of the church. They need to evaluate the mental picture of the church they have developed over the years. They need fresh experiences in all phases of the church's life. They also need a chance to compare their picture of the church with the church's official statements of purpose.

ACTIVITIES TO BUILD UNDERSTANDING (SELECT ONE OR MORE)

(1) Study several statements by the church about its nature and mission. This task requires adult help. One young person with his adult advisor or a small class needs to read through several of the church's statements and explore their meanings. A simple way to structure the discussion is to make two cumulative lists as a group works: (1) what the church is, and (2) what the church does. Also take time to define troublesome words (example: "I believe in . . . the holy *catholic* church" in the Apostle's Creed). It may be helpful to ask students to put parts of a statement into their own words. Choose appropriate parts of the following:

> creeds/confessions (be sure to include modern as well as older ones)
> catechisms
> denominational statements of purpose
> local congregational statements of purpose
> scripture (you may want to revise this list to reflect your denomination's stance)
>> Matthew 25:27-40   I Corinthians 12:4-7
>> Matthew 28:18-20   I Corinthians 12:12-13
>> Acts 2:42   II Corinthians 8:1-5

(2) After studying the nature and mission of the church, a student states his or her own ideas about what the church should be and do by doing one of the following:

—making up a verbal or written definition of the word "church."

—describing "my ideal church" and outlining what it would be like and what it would do.

—creating a collage describing what he or she thinks the church should be or do.

(3) A small group can follow up study about the nature and mission of the church with an opportunity to share personal ideas and feelings about the church. Ask each person to rank the items on the following list in order of importance in their opinion. Number from one to six, with one being most important and six being least important. Stress the fact that there are no right or wrong answers on this. After all have decided their ranking, compare lists. Discuss the reasons individuals have for ranking items as they did.

Two or three people will be able to compare and discuss most of their lists. Larger groups may prefer to focus only on what each person ranked highest and lowest.

Rank the following from one to six, in order of importance *to you*.

_____ have beautiful worship services

_____ keep nice buildings and grounds

_____ help church members learn more about what it means to follow Jesus

_____ tell people outside the church about Jesus

_____ feed the hungry, welcome strangers, clothe the naked, take care of the sick, visit prisoners

_____ church members love each other and have fun together

(4) Each young person prepares a scrapbook about his church following a given outline. Outlines can vary. One outline might ask students to provide information about different groups within the church. (Be sure to include the congregation's participation in the "larger church.") Another outline might focus on types of church activity such as worship, international mission, and nurture. All outlines need to include suggestions on how to get the information for each section. If several students are working on scrapbooks, each one may use the same outline, or they may use different outlines. Sharing results can produce lively discussion and comparisons.

(5) Students compare what they learned about the nature and mission of the church from creeds and scripture with what they found out about their congregation by making scrapbooks. For discussion ask:

—Which of the items on your lists of what the church is and does are found in your congregation?

—Which, if any, are missing?

—In what ways is your congregation strongest (like your congregation says it should be)?

—What do you think your congregation needs to work more on in order to live up to its calling?

(6) Carry out a set number of projects such as those suggested below. Report on each project and discuss it with an adult leader.

_____ pack clothes for shipping to missions

_____ go visiting with minister or other Christian leader

_____ visit a church-sponsored institution (nursing home, children's home, halfway house)

_____ read an approved biography of a Christian leader

_____ join in any of the congregation's mission projects (ride along on Meals on Wheels, go along with tutors)

(7) Check your denominational materials for other activities that help youth understand what the church is and does.

TASK #2

KNOW AND APPRECIATE THE CONGREGATION'S WORSHIP WAYS

Public and private worship are the heart of the Christian life. Therefore it is essential for an individual to understand and appreciate the way a congregation worships together. The order of worship should be understood. The regularly used prayers, creeds, and songs should be known and understood. Individuals also need to develop a private worship life. If this is new, very specific suggestions are needed. More experienced youth may need introduction to more mature devotional materials.

ACTIVITIES TO BUILD UNDERSTANDING (SELECT ONE OR MORE)

(1) Require regular attendance at Sunday congregational worship.

(2) Youth fill out "Worshipsheets" for a set number of worship services. Share and discuss findings with leader and other youth (see sample "Worshipsheet").

(3) Youth fill out a "Sermon Worksheet" on a specific sermon. Meet with the preacher shortly after the sermon to check answers, discussing the sermon content and how to listen to sermons (see sample "Sermon Worksheet").

(4) With worship leader, youth discuss the meaning of each part of worship listed on the Sunday worship bulletin.

(5) Youth plan Sunday morning worship service with the minister. Select and/or create appropriate hymns, prayers, and creeds. Discuss sermon ideas for the set scripture passages. Youth may also be involved in the leadership of the service, or may participate as members of the congregation.

(6) Require youth to practice daily personal worship. Students for whom this is a new experience will need a guide. There are many excellent daily devotional guides—some especially for youth. Check in regularly to learn how youth are progressing in this discipline. Openly discuss preferences for time of day, place, and kinds of prayer. Identify common difficulties and ways of coping with them.

(7) Check your denominational materials for other activities that help youth participate more fully in the congregation's worship and help youth develop their private worship life.

SAMPLE

WORSHIPSHEET

1. Which hymn today was your favorite? Why?

2. In your own words, briefly tell the message of that hymn.

3. What scripture was the sermon based on?

4. What was the main point of the sermon?

5. List at least two things you prayed about in worship today.

6. What was the main theme of this worship service?

7. What in this worship service meant the most to you personally? Why?

SAMPLE

SERMON WORKSHEET

In this sermon, three stories are told about forgiveness. For each story—list the main characters, and tell what they had to forgive.

(1)

(2)

(3)

The sermon mentions two kinds of faith it takes to forgive. In your own words, describe these two kinds of faith:

(1)

(2)

The sermon mentions several scriptures about forgiveness. Answer the following questions about these scriptures:

(1) Who did Joseph forgive?

(2) Where was Jesus when he said: "Forgive them, Father! They don't know what they are doing."?

(3) Who said: "Never take revenge, my friends, but instead let God's anger do it."?

(4) What does God promise to those who "forgive others the wrongs they have done to you"?

In the space below, tell what was the most important thing for you in this sermon.

TASK #3

UNDERSTAND THE ROLE AND SIGNIFICANCE OF THE SACRAMENTS

Though the sacraments are part of the church's regular worship life, they merit particular attention at confirmation because many youth will be baptized or participate in their first communion at this time. The Lord's Supper is probably quite familiar to them. Baptism may require careful attention to the difference in infant baptism and believer's baptism in some denominations. Any young person to be baptized should be introduced to the questions that will be asked during baptism.

ACTIVITIES TO BUILD UNDERSTANDING (SELECT ONE OR MORE)

Lord's Supper

(1) Youth plan a communion service for the homebound and help the pastor lead the service for homebound members of the congregation. (This is an excellent opportunity for older members to share their faith as they tell youth what communion means to them.)

(2) Youth with adult worship leaders plan a communion service for the entire congregation. Read through and discuss the set readings and prayers for communion. Prepare the bread and wine for the service. (Some youth may even provide homemade bread!)

(3) Study communion hymns. Together adults and youth flip through the section of the hymnbook with hymns for communion. Identify familiar hymns. Point out favorites to each other. Let individuals explain why they like or dislike some of the hymns. Answer questions about particular hymns or words. Then focus on one or two communion hymns. Read all verses and help students put the messages into their own words. Identify what the song says about the sacrament, discussing what it means to sing those words in worship. A musical young person might learn to play one or more of the hymns.

(4) Check denominational study materials for other activities that help youth explore communion. Many denominations provide exceptional filmstrips and movies about communion. These may be available free from area offices.

Baptism

(1) Students put questions that are asked of them in the baptism rite into their own words and discuss the significance of answering those questions.

(2) Students interview members of their congregation to learn the story of their baptism and what it means to them. The adult leader's task is to identify the adults to be interviewed. These adults should include people baptized at a variety of points in life and in different situations. If your church practices infant baptism, interview both an adult baptized as an infant and a parent who had an infant baptized. Ask both about their experience and understanding of infant baptism. Select people whose understanding of

baptism reflects that of your denomination and who can express themselves clearly to teen-agers. The basic questions to be asked are:

    —What is the story of your baptism?
    —What did your baptism mean to you at that time?
    —What does your baptism mean to you today?

Older youth may conduct the interviews on their own. Younger teens will learn more if they conduct such interviews with adult support. After the interviews, share results and discuss what can be learned from all the stories. It may be interesting to read the story of Jesus' baptism, discuss its significance for Jesus at different times in his life, and compare that significance with the baptism for the congregation members interviewed.

(3) Check denominational study materials for activities that help youth explore baptism. Many denominations provide unusually fine filmstrips and movies about baptism. These may be available free from area denominational offices.

TASK #4

KNOW HOW THE CHURCH IS GOVERNED

To be effective, members of an organization must know how the organization operates. Who makes what kind of decisions? Where do you take different problems? How do things get done? Church members should know how their church gets things done.

ACTIVITIES TO BUILD UNDERSTANDING (SELECT ONE OR MORE)

(1) Youth visit meetings of the official bodies of their congregation and fill out a worksheet as they observe the meeting (see sample worksheet for Presbyterian youth observing a Session meeting). After the meeting, youth discuss what they learned and compare their answers with an adult.

(2) Under adult leadership, youth study organizational charts and learn the names of the people in each body in their congregation.

(3) Each youth interviews a church officer about their work. An adult may need to pre-plan questions with young interviewers, so that they will get the information they need about the officer's work.

(4) If your denomination has area decision-making bodies (districts, associations, presbyteries), visit a meeting (or part of a meeting) of that body.

(5) Visit area denominational offices to learn about the church's work at that level. Call ahead so that someone is prepared to give your small group the tour and introduce you to the staff.

(6) Check denominational, church school, and even officer training materials for useful resources. Many denominations produce filmstrips on church government that provide basic information. Such filmstrips can launch students successfully into the preceding activities. Your area office may have one to loan free.

SAMPLE

SESSION THINK SHEET

Cross Road's Session has twelve ruling elders and one teaching elder.

The teaching elder is _____.

There are _____ ruling elders here tonight.

Who is the Clerk of our Session? _____.

What is the Clerk's job? _____

_____

At each meeting the Session hears reports from each committee that it oversees. Listen as reports are called for and write the name of each committee below:

1. _____

2. _____

3. _____

Below is a list of some things the *Book of Church Order* says a Session should do. Star each one they do while you are here.

1. express concern about the Christian growth of all church members.
2. record baptisms and welcome children to the Lord's Table.
3. confirm people.
4. dismiss people who have moved to other churches.
5. examine and install new elders and deacons.
6. oversee the work of the deacons.
7. plan for the church school.
8. set times and places for worship services.
9. approve special offerings.
10. carry out the orders of higher courts.
11. select elders to go to meetings of Presbytery and Synod.

TASK #5

UNDERSTAND THE BASICS OF THE CHRISTIAN FAITH

This is the most important and the hardest part of the job. The task is to pull together all that each young person has learned and experienced of the faith. In the process we must listen as youth express their understandings and then challenge them to grow in faith where they need it. We need to help them compare their faith to the church's standards

ACTIVITIES TO BUILD UNDERSTANDING (SELECT ONE OR MORE)

(1) Each youth reads a gospel (Mark is the shortest and easiest for youth to understand) and discusses it with the adult leaders and/or group. (*Translating the Good News Through Teaching Activities* by Donald Griggs describes several ways that one or more can think about the message or faith of an entire gospel.)

(2) With adult help, youth study some of the big words with which Christians express our faith. Many of these words are used frequently with the assumption that everyone knows what they mean. Unfortunately, many people who grow up in the church learn how to use the words without really understanding their meaning.

sin	salvation	grace
forgiveness	discipleship	vocation
eternal life	judgment	resurrection
faith	believe	

- Select no more than three or four of the key words in the list above. Select words that together summarize the Christian faith. (Example: sin, salvation, and discipleship).

- Together look up each word in the Bible (using a concordance), creeds, catechisms, dictionaries, and other sources. If you know of passages from short stories, novels, or study books that relate to a word, read them together. As you read, discuss how each passage relates to the key words.

- Help students define each word in their own words based on their studies.

- Students compose one or two sentences using all the studied words in a way that (1) summarizes the faith, and (2) shows the relationship of the words.

(3) With adult help, study one creed or confession that summarizes the Christian faith. Discuss the meaning of each phrase or section. Together look up words with unclear meanings. Help students put especially difficult phrases into their own words. (You may want to work on a modern creed that speaks in language youth more readily understand. Or you may want to select a traditional creed that is frequently used in the church's worship, so that youth can use it with fuller understanding. Whichever creed or confession you select, build on the students' understanding of the Christian message and faith.)

(4) Study and learn the catechism. (Some denominations place a high value on memorizing their catechism. Others prefer that students study and discuss it. And catechisms are no longer used in some

denominations. No matter how a catechism is used, the goal is that youth *understand* what is asked and answered, rather than parroting a perfect but meaningless response.)

(5) Check your denominational materials for exercises designed to help students summarize the Christian faith with increasing understanding.

MAKING THE DECISION

Each of the other blocks of confirmation enable the young person to evaluate some part of the Christian life. As they work through these activities, youth will begin making their decision or will deepen their commitment to the decision they have already made. But finally, one or two carefully chosen activities must put before each person—the decision. It is important that a free decision is offered. Young people need to be offered the option of deciding not to be confirmed and to be promised that their decision will be respected. Without this option, the decision has no integrity.

Each person has a reason for deferring his or her decision. Some youth who take Christian commitment most seriously will work through a confirmation program but defer making their commitment, feeling they are not ready. Other youth may never explain their reasons for deferring. But the congregation that honors that decision to defer and offers continuing love to those young people leaves the door open for a different decision at a later date.

ACTIVITIES THAT FOCUS THE DECISION AND CELEBRATE CONFIRMATION (SELECT ONE OR MORE)

(1) Each youth creates a personal statement of faith using the method of expression with which the young person is most comfortable.

write a creed

write an essay

compose a song or poem

put together some pictures or slides as a collage or slide show (with or without words or music)

others:

It will be helpful to give youth a short list of topics—why Jesus is important, what they think about God and the church, and how being Christian affects everyday living.

(2) With adult guidance, youth study the questions to be asked in the confirmation ritual. Putting the questions and answers into their own words is usually helpful. In some churches, reworded questions can be used in the ritual. Discuss the effect that answering the questions positively would have.

(3) Youth to be confirmed plan the confirmation service with the minister. Write prayers and select readings and hymns that are especially meaningful. The service might include statements of faith (activity #1).

(4) Some denominations require potential members to meet with the ruling board to answer specific questions before they are publicly received into membership during worship. Youth to be confirmed in these churches may plan a presentation/report to this body. The presentation outlines what they have done in their program and may include their statements of faith (activity #1).

ANOTHER OPTION

Seven small churches of the same denomination in North Carolina created a cooperative confirmation program where they combined all of their resources to provide an experience none of the churches could offer alone. A total of twenty-three youth from the seven churches met on seven Wednesday afternoons after school and went on two retreats. Each session focused on a different aspect of the Christian life under the leadership of one of the four ministers. Because each minister planned only two sessions, each one worked hard to develop interesting activities. The session on church history was a tour through four appropriately decorated rooms where the group experienced church life during different periods of the church's history. To learn church policy, the young people became an imaginary church board responding to a variety of situations according to church order. On one retreat they created an imaginary church, planned its budget, designed its building, called a pastor, and faced a few crises. Then, the group created a video-taped documentary about their church. The tape was one part of their presentation at a dinner meeting with their parents and church boards when they were examined for membership in their respective churches.

Every cooperative program is unique. The common thread is that each one combines the best leadership and resources available in all of the involved congregations to make confirmation a rich and meaningful experience.

CHAPTER 5

BUILDING A COMPLETE YOUTH MINISTRY

A congregation's youth ministry is a complex whole made up of several parts. The parts differ from church to church. Some of the parts are church school class, recognition of graduates, confirmation, and youth groups. Each part is important. But no one part can be a congregation's total youth ministry in itself.

Paul's description of the church as a human body in I Corinthians 12 could easily apply to a church's youth ministry. To make a rough paraphrase: Youth ministry is not complete in only one youth program. The church school class cannot say to the choir, "Because you do not study scripture, you are not really doing youth ministry as I am." Nor can a church sports team say, "Because I do not provide worship, I offer nothing to youth ministry." Youth ministry is more than just study, worship, or service. If youth ministry were just a church school class, where would youth find opportunities to be the church today? Or if it were just confirmation, where would youth be able to build friendships with adult Christians, which over the years often shape young lives? No—all parts are necessary for the health of the whole. Each has a different function, but all work together to meet every need of the congregation's youth.

The whole body of each congregation's youth ministry is unique. It is composed of parts chosen and shaped by that congregation to meet specific needs. In a healthy ministry—all the parts are carefully planned to fit together precisely and to work together in harmony. The church school teachers, youth advisors, parents, and adult leaders are part of a team that coordinates their individual labors toward a common goal.

Building this kind of completeness takes a little work. The first task is to develop a common vision of (1) what the congregation is trying to do in youth ministry, and (2) what each part contributes to the work of the whole. This need not be an arduous process. In most churches an unspoken, unwritten vision is already widely accepted. So the task is to put the vision into words, saying aloud the function of each part of the ministry.

The following exercise is designed to enable congregations to do this task and in the process give the whole ministry a tune-up so that it functions more effectively. A minister, teacher, or advisor can learn a lot by working through the exercise alone. However, the exercise is really a job for a group. So gather adults involved in all parts of your youth ministry; invite interested parents; and maybe include a few mature older youth. The broader the participation, the clearer will be your results and the easier it will be to implement ideas that grow from your work together.

To do this exercise, you will need a large chalk board or long sheet of chart paper.

STEP 1. On one side of the paper, print in a column the six needs of youth described in chapter 1. Leave space between each of the items so that the column fills the length of the paper. If your group includes people who are encountering these needs for the first time, briefly introduce these needs individually and as a whole.

STEP 2. On the other side of the paper, print in a column a list of all parts of your youth ministry. This list should include all significant parts of your congregation's work with young people. Select items from the "Parts of Complete Youth Ministries" list in this chapter. Add parts that are not on the list. Leave space between items so that the column fills the length of the paper. Leave as much space as possible between this column and the column listing needs.

STEP 3. Draw lines connecting each part of youth ministry to the need(s) met intentionally in your congregation. Do not draw lines to needs that *might* be met in a congregation, but only to needs that *are* met in your congregation. Do not draw lines to needs that are met by accident. (For example, it would be hard to name any part that does not make young people feel loved.) Draw connecting lines only to those parts that consciously and specifically attempt to make youth feel loved.

As you draw these lines, make sure it is clear how many lines are converging on each item. (As more and more lines are drawn, the space between the columns will begin looking like impressionistic string art.)

STEP 4. Count the lines converging on each need and mark that number beside each need. (You may want to circle the number or write it in a different color to make it stand out.)

STEP 5. Count the lines converging on each part. Mark that number beside each part of your youth ministry. (Again, you may want to circle the number or write it in a different color.)

STEP 6. Estimate the percentage of your congregation's youth who participate in each part of your youth ministry. Mark that number near the part. (Yet another color might differentiate these percentages from counts of converging lines.)

STEP 7. Put up another sheet of newsprint and title it "Work To Be Done."

STEP 8. You have now gathered lots of information about the completeness of your youth ministry. Use the following questions to evaluate this information. As you talk, identify specific work or changes that would improve your ministry. Record these on the "Work To Be Done" list.

—On which needs do you focus? Why?
—Which need(s) receive least attention? Why?
—Which need(s) need more attention than they now receive? Should any receive less attention?

SAMPLE

The following is the chart and "Work To Be Done" list of a one hundred member church that includes about ten junior and senior high students and another five older youth who shared in some youth activities.

PARTS   NEEDS

80% church school classes ③ ────────── ⑤ a group in which to be loved

75% youth fellowship ③ ────────── ② friendships with adult Christians

85% softball team ① ────────── ③ encouragement to think . . .

85% youth choir ② ────────── ② chance to be the church TODAY

50% summer day camp ③ ────────── ① exposure to the richness and diversity of the whole church

25% co-op Jr. High Fellowship ① ────────── ② to see selves as Christians

85% congregational worship ②

WORK TO BE DONE

—love them a little less and challenge them a little more.

—focus on being the church in fellowship—there's more to "being the church" than worship.

—get a hardworking registrar for camp and do better promotion—we may need to offer easier transportation.

—find out more about co-op Jr. High Fellowship so we can support it or withdraw from it.

—find out about our denomination's camps and conferences—encourage attendance—talk to budget committee about camperships.

—What changes in the current parts could result in meeting needs more completely?

—Refer to the "Parts of Youth Ministry" list. What new parts could your church add in order to meet needs more completely?

—Compare the "percentage of participation" figures to the "needs met" figures for each "part."

—If any part that meets many needs has low percentage participation, identify ways to increase participation.

—Identify parts that meet so few needs and get so little participation that they should be discontinued.

STEP 9. Do not throw away your charts! Use the "Work To Be Done" chart to check up on progress on the tasks identified. You may also want to refer to the big chart throughout the year.

Parts of Complete Youth Ministries

church school class(es)
youth group(s)
confirmation program
encouragement to attend church camps and conferences
vocational guidance
introduction to church colleges
(youth) choir
congregational worship
youth trips
cooperative youth events
cooperative youth groups
Vacation Bible School
graduation recognition
sports teams
Christian youth magazine subscription
service on church boards and committees
Others:

This exercise is particularly designed as an evaluation or tune-up tool. If things seem to have fallen apart, it is one way to begin putting them together again. If things are going fairly well, it can be a good check-up. The exercise can point out strong points (take time to celebrate them!) and identify deficiencies (identify ways to work on them). A church developing youth ministry for the first time could adapt the exercise to select parts of their blossoming youth ministry and designate the needs each part should meet.

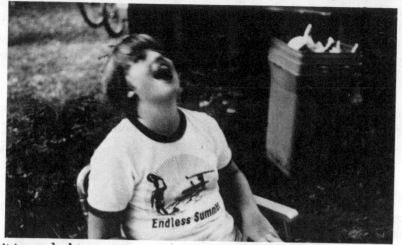

However it is used, this exercise emphasizes the need for some planning and coordination of efforts in youth ministry on a regular basis. How this is done varies from church to church: some churches assign the task to a committee; others handle the work less formally. The following describes ways that several churches have assigned the task of oversight and coordination of youth ministry.

(1) **Christian Education Committee.** Many churches assign responsibility for a church's overall education ministry to one committee called the Christian Education Committee, Strengthening the Church Committee, Nurture Committee, or a similar name. In many churches this group can do the work of overseeing youth ministry. These committees generally include people who are familiar with and active in youth ministry. It is important to keep them up-to-date and thinking. Much of this can be done as part of monthly meetings as they coordinate plans, respond to problems and opportunities, and ascertain that what is going on is in line with the accepted vision of youth ministry.

But occasionally, the committee needs to set aside time to focus on youth ministry. Some committees set aside one meeting each year to evaluate what they have been doing and do long-range planning for the coming year. Often they invite adult leaders of youth and youth to participate in this meeting. These meetings clarify the church's vision of what it is doing in youth ministry and set the tone for the year.

(2) **Youth Sub-Committee of Christian Education Committee.** Larger churches that are currently ministering to a small number of youth may have such a large and complex education ministry to the whole congregation that the Christian Education Committee must create sub-committees for each aspect of their ministry. In such cases a youth ministries sub-committee might be formed under the supervision of the Christian Education Committee. This sub-committee should include all adult leaders of all parts of the congregation's youth ministry and may include one or two mature youth. In regular meetings (perhaps quarterly) the committee shares plans, evaluates what is being done in terms of needs to be met, coordinates activities as needed, solves problems, and considers new possibilities. Their work is reported to the Christian Education Committee.

(3) **Annual Youth Ministry Meetings.** In smaller churches that do their work more informally, a committee may be unnecessary. Instead, all involved and interested people may be invited to an annual meeting at which the last year's work is evaluated in terms of the accepted vision, and directions are set

for the coming year. The group may work through an exercise such as the one in this chapter, see a film about youth ministry, or otherwise explore youth ministry in broad terms. But the group will also decide what time the fellowship will meet, ask if there are youth ready for confirmation, enlist fellowship advisors, and handle other business.

The critical thing about using this plan is that someone has to call the meetings. Even if the meetings are always in early September, someone has to set the date, get the word out, and moderate the meeting. The minister, church school superintendent, a designated member of the ruling board, or someone else in the congregation may be assigned the task. Who does it is less important than that someone is clearly and publicly responsible.

The reason that the ruling board of the church is not mentioned for this work is that churches of all sizes have too much business to leave the ruling board the time needed to do this work. Therefore some other group must do the detailed work and *report regularly* to the board. These regular reports are required in many denominations because the board (by church law) has to approve what is done. But it is even more important because it keeps board members (who unfortunately may have little contact with youth) informed about the congregation's youth ministry. The reports educate the members so that they can become advocates for youth ministry.

A FINAL WORD

The old preacher said, "Tell them what you're going to tell them. Tell them. Then tell them what you told them." So, I'll say it one more time.

There is no one RIGHT WAY to do youth ministry. In fact, there is no one right way to do youth ministry in your congregation. What works in one church may not work in another. What worked in your church last year may be all wrong this year.

Th only right way to do youth ministry is to offer your particular young people the loving care they need and opportunities to grow in the understanding and living of the Christian faith. The only way to do this is for a group of caring adults to make it their business to know their young people and to take responsibility for creating ministries that are appropriate to their youths' needs and potentials. This book offers those caring adults some tools with which to do the job.

There are no shortcuts to avoid the hard work of creating and carrying out youth ministry. Real youth ministry requires commitment and hard work on the part of several adults. But there is something very "grace-full" about it. Part of the grace is in the close relationships with young Christians. Part of it is in the growing they force us to do as we minister to them. And part of it is in the mutual support and caring among the adults working together. The work, although hard and frustrating at times—is bearable, worthwhile, and even saving.

So, roll up your sleeves . . .

Pick up your tools . . .

And get to work!